Art In My Heart

The Power of Watercolor Mandala Making

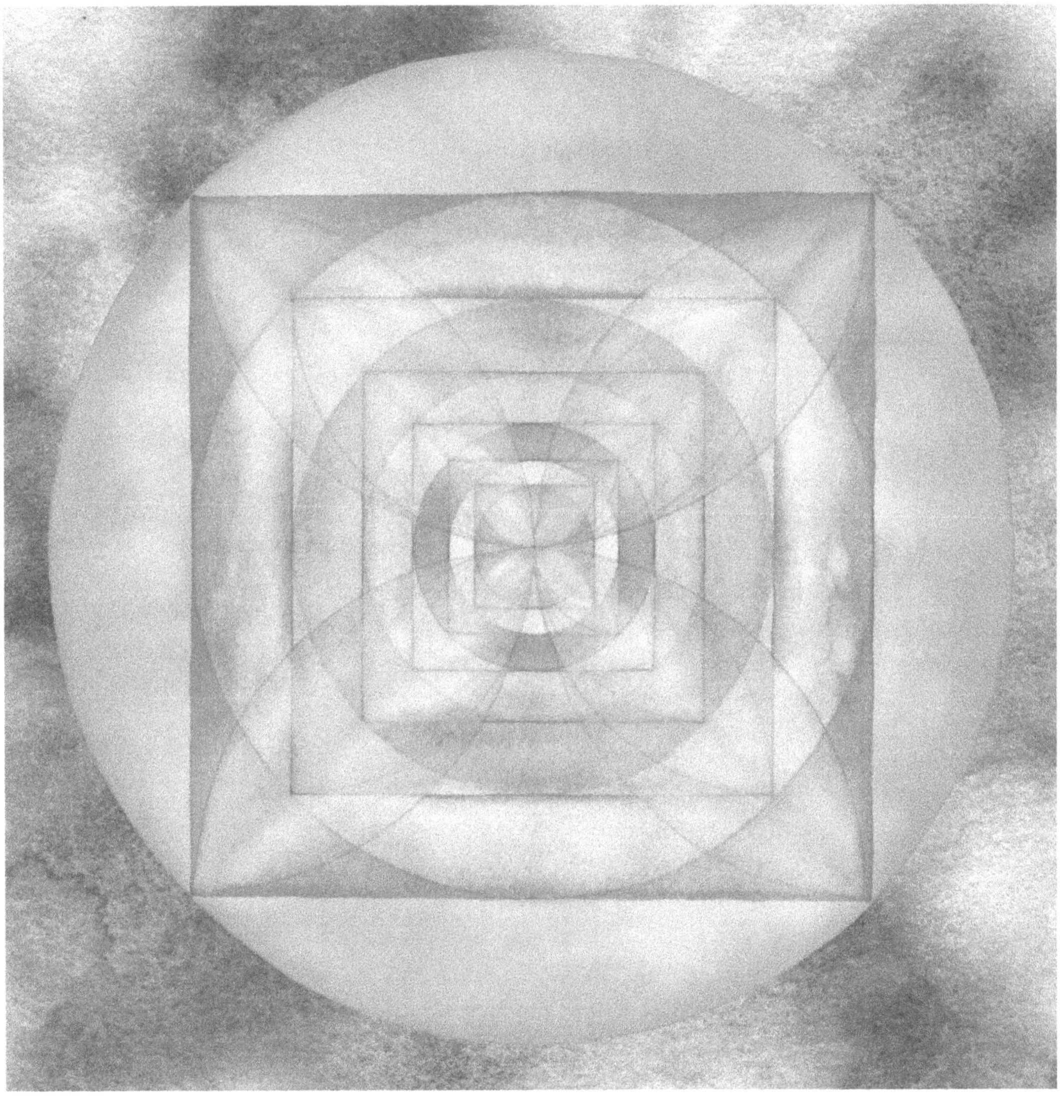

Michele Faia

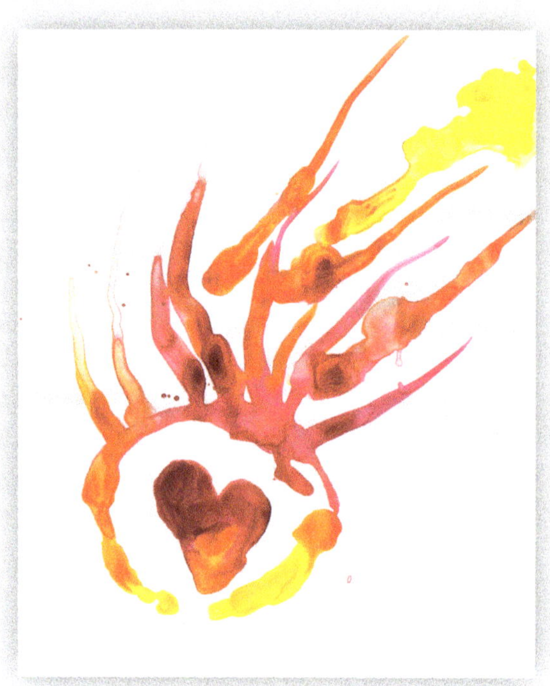

DEDICATED TO ALL THOSE
WHO HAVE KEPT THE FLAME ALIVE IN MY HEART

Art in My Heart; The Power of Watercolor Mandala Making
Michele Faia—1st Edition

Published by Michele Faia
Aptos, California

Creative Direction and Design: Don Faia
Design and Production: Kim Ferrell
Dedication Page Art: Don Faia
Front Cover Art: *Life's Purpose*, Michele Faia
Front Cover Production: Tom Dill

ISBN # 978-0-9799354-0-4

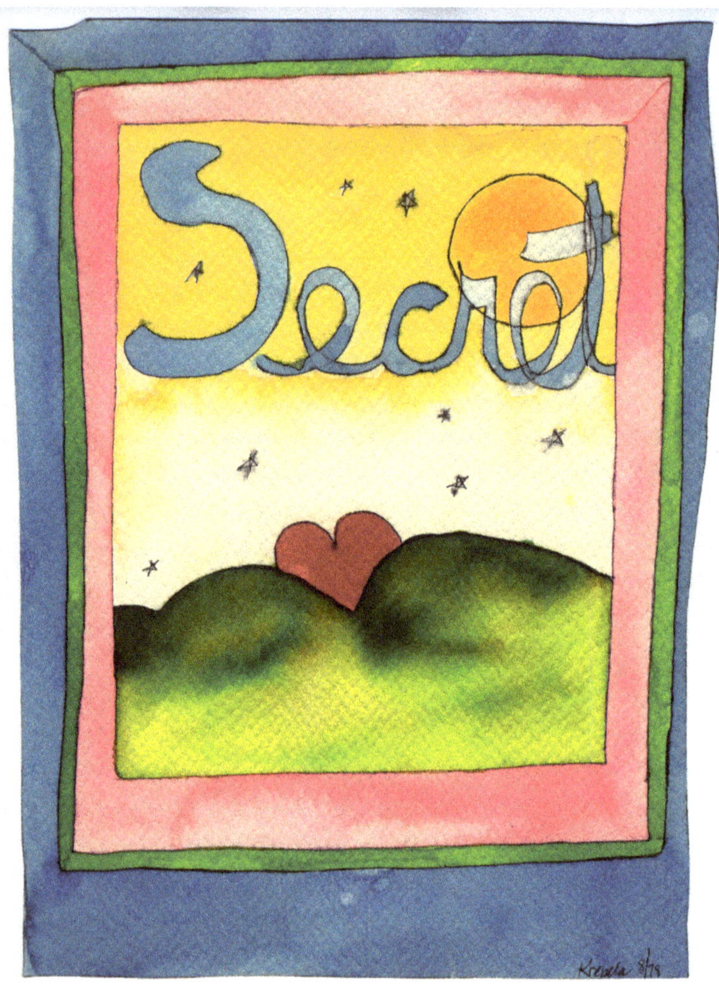

My Secret, watercolor dyes, black felt pen

Sacred Circles

WHEN I FIRST STARTED writing this book I thought it would simply be a "how to" book on painting watercolor mandalas. Mandalas, or sacred circles, have been used for centuries to assist meditation. I had been encouraged by my students to write a book based on the teaching technique I had developed from years of painting mandalas myself. But I had not included in the original text what a tremendous impact painting these little circle paintings (mandala in Sanskrit means circle, or center) had on my heart and my life. The whole story was really the personal transformation which had occurred for me through mandala painting. I knew I had to go deeper into the details of that transformation. Opening myself up felt good on the one hand, but the vulnerability of it really scared me.

Because of the amazing experiences I had with mandalas, the only choice seemed to be to jump in. As I wrote in my journal, "It's a story. Let the story unfold. It's a story about your heart. Let it be told." So, I have jumped into the telling.

The mandala became a symbol for the calm, quiet place within myself. In painting mandalas I centered, healed, made peace with myself and re-emerged more alive and whole. I found the well of my creativity and spirit. I found my heart. It was truly magical.

Why Mandalas?

Several years ago I was experiencing terrible chronic fatigue and I didn't know what the cause was, nor did the numerous doctors and health practitioners I consulted. My husband and I had moved back to Santa Cruz County which was considered a very nurturing place to heal. I needed peace, wanted health, and was searching for answers. I began seeing a body worker to deal with the anger, frustration, hopelessness and depression that resulted from having what I was told was an "incurable" condition. With her encouragement I began to paint the "colorful and very visual" images I got during our intense sessions.

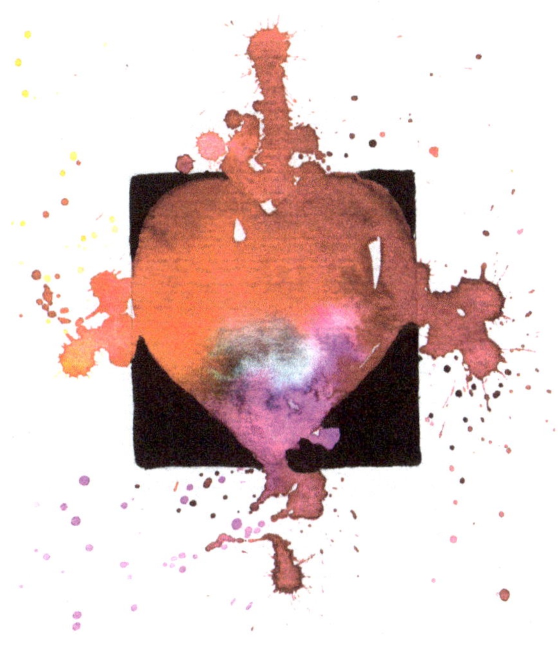

Exploding Heart, watercolor

I painted this in the first few months of painting mandalas. I do consider it a mandala; symmetrical and circular (within the square) with an implied center. I continued to paint hearts for many years. Here I felt my heart was so full of withheld emotions it was exploding.

Weekly I brought in paintings full of hearts and tears to show her. My actual inner artwork, however, had started years before with very personal drawings and paintings of my heart. They were expressions of my emotions, and I loved doing them. With them I felt I had found a place within myself where I *was* truly capable of being creative and expressive. That discovery brought me incredible joy. One such painting, *My Secret,* was of a vision I had of the dawning of that creative place inside myself. I hid my work then, thinking it was childish and not really "art."

In the bodywork sessions I felt safe again to express my heart, as in *Exploding Heart*. It was during that time that I felt a very strong desire to paint mandalas. A friend was drawing mandalas and I was fascinated and attracted to them. I wanted to try making them as well and began to search for a way I could learn. Later I realized that those in the process of going through a healing or life transition, as I was, gravitate to mandalas.

And so, with mandalas, I began a spiritual journey to the center of myself, to my heart, and this is the story of that journey. I share the process with the hope that the healing it has brought me will continue, and will also, be of benefit to others.

AN EXCITING JOURNEY

This is a "how to" guide for journeying to your own heart by painting watercolor mandalas. There are many reasons people are attracted to watercolor mandalas. You may just want to play, or to try watercolor for the first time, or to express yourself. You may want to relax and have fun exploring your inner world and let go of the need to paint or draw perfectly. You may want to paint as a meditation. You can do any or all of these. Everyone, yes everyone, can do mandalas. With mandalas I have learned to play more, to judge

myself less, to let go, to heal, to know myself, to express myself, to surprise myself, to nurture myself, and to love myself. I have begun to learn what the "self" is, which, according to Carl Jung, is the archetype of wholeness. And in addition to all of that, my painting skills have improved and my creativity and imagination have really come alive. It has been an exciting journey!

CREATE YOUR SACRED SPACE

Imagine now inscribing a circle around yourself, and putting your own heart at the center, in the place of honor. You have now created a space, a sacred circle, in which to begin your sacred work. Let's turn inward and start to explore what treasures you will find there.

"When we attune ourselves to a mandala, with the right kind of concentration, we experience a change in consciousness. Meditating on a mandala takes us on a journey into our wise centre which is in harmony with the cosmos."[2]

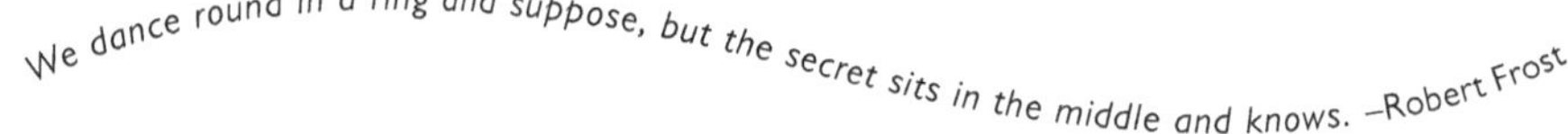

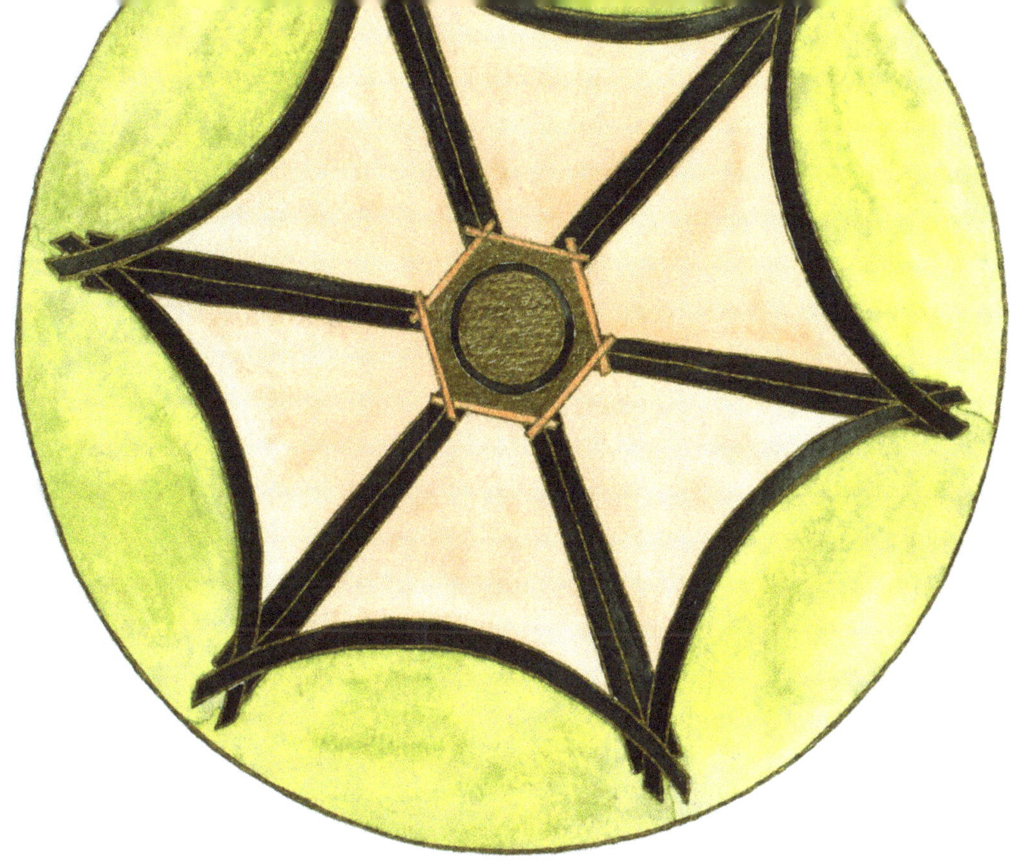

MAKING MANDALAS EASY AND FUN

HOW DO I BEGIN?

Until you actually have the experience of doing a mandala, it can be difficult to understand what they really are. In teaching others how to do personal mandalas, and then subsequently putting it all down in this book, I have concentrated on how to get started quickly and easily, while having fun with the process. This is the way I learned and it unfolded for me in a very natural and easy way. Basically, the process taught me, and I will show you how it did and how you can make it work for you. It has a wonderful mystery-like quality as it reveals itself. The beauty of this is that your own process will be leading and teaching you. Once I show you a few guidelines at the beginning, you can continue following them or create your own path for teaching yourself. You are your own best teacher, so trust that. So now you are at the point of wanting to do a mandala, or at least you are very curious about them. You wouldn't have picked up this book if you weren't

interested, and something, you may not know what, has drawn you to them. I shall assume you are ready and willing just like I was. "Now what?" I had asked, with both apprehension and curiosity. "How do I begin?"

The initial inspiration for doing mandalas came from my garden when I noticed that most blooming flowers were mandalas. And, it was from an actual physical experience of feeling like a flower during a bodywork session, that I began to understand the concept. I tried painting my first circle painting, *Myself As A Flower*, and called it a "flower mandala." This experience helped me to know how to proceed. With it I discovered the joy, surprise and empowerment of going to the center of myself and representing what I saw and felt, from within. All this was aided, in ways I did not initially understand, by working within the circular format. What I believe occurred was that the circling, inward focus opened my heart. A friend suggested that this painting was a depiction of my heart chakra. Chakras are energy centers in the

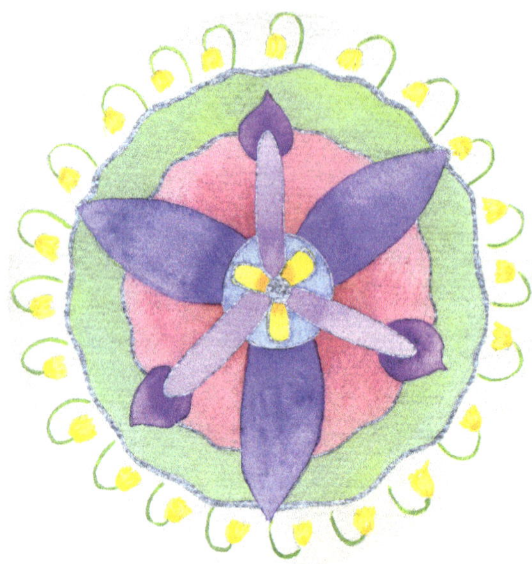

Flower of Myself, watercolor, silver pen

I wondered if I could create a mandala by following
the design of a flower. I gave it a try. First I drew, then
painted, imagining what my inner flower would look like from
above if it were fully opened and blooming. This process
is a very good way to begin doing mandalas.

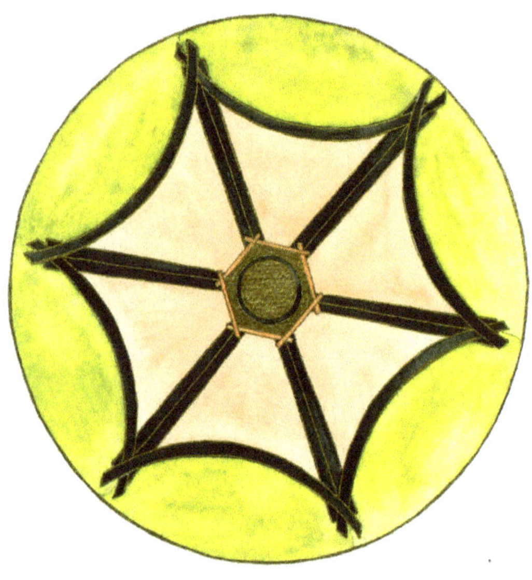

Sacred Space: A Place To Rest, watercolor, gold pen

I consider this to be my first true mandala. It came from
a vision I had of a place I wanted to go and rest. I tried to
approximate what I had seen, drawing it first but feeling
awkward and unsure of what I was doing. I felt better and
better as I focused on expressing my feelings of peace,
serenity and sacredness. When I finished painting I
felt fulfilled, centered and whole. I knew I was
beginning to learn the power of the mandala.

subtle body seen in Eastern art as spinning and unfolding flowers. I think my friend was right, it was my heart energy. This was such a wonderful experience for me, I have since used the flower mandala as one of the first processes we do in class. See Chapter Five, "The Flower of Myself."

FROM MANDALA MAKING TO MANDALA TEACHING

Defined, a mandala is "a spiritual tool which is used to assist concentration and meditation. It is usually a symmetrical and circular image which can be either a purely geometrical composition or a figurative one, and is said to be a spiritual diagram of the universe showing the process by which an individual can return to their original source."[3] So in my process of trying to learn about what a mandala was, I had opened my heart energy with the "flower mandala." I was now ready "to go beyond the antipasto," as one friend joked. Not sure that I had really done a true mandala in *Myself As a Flower*, I was still looking for a more complete experience of the process.

The inspiration for that process came again from a bodywork session in which I saw an Asian-like circular, sacred space surrounded by green, peaceful grass. This seemed to be good material for a mandala. I drew an outline approximating the design I had seen, and then painted it, holding to the circle motif as in *Sacred Space: A Place to Rest*. A strange thing then happened. A place of total clarity seemed to open up within my head, a great calm came over me, and I heard: "You know what to do, you know how to do it. Go teach." I was not a trained watercolor teacher, art history yes, but not watercolor. And although this was my first mandala, I knew with complete certainty this was what I was to do.

I must say something about this mandala. Years later I came across a Shinto shrine which stirred in me the feelings I'd experienced while painting this mandala. The shrine represented the crossing of a threshold which separated the secular world from the sacred world of the gods. In other words, a sort of gateway to sacred space—just what my mandala was about. This has always been an exciting and fascinating part of doing mandalas, discovering that they have a much deeper meaning than what I originally thought.

This first mandala was an unparalleled inner experience for me and it was the beginning, the gateway to my sacred space. I wanted to know more about them and so I began a search, finding mandalas in Carl Jung's writings and in only one book in the public library. What I remember from the book, *Mandala* by Jose and Miriam Argueles, was that mandalas had three basic properties: "a center, symmetry, cardinal points."[4] After that, however, I just wasn't sure about them, so I made the decision to let go and let the process teach me by experience. This was new for me. I had always thought I preferred to learn "by-the-book."

After a few weeks of painting and learning from mandalas, I proposed a class to the local Community Education Office and began to teach a beginning watercolor mandala class that summer. The class evolved, some students stayed for years and others became mandala teachers themselves. One English woman, who became a very special friend, began teaching mandalas at 83 and taught until she was 89! See Lane Cara Shaw's *My First Mandala*.

Having been ill for several years and unable to work full-time, I watched myself slowly become stronger as I continued to paint mandalas. My students as well made many personal changes and we all had fun making "art," most for the first time since childhood. We made art not as is found in galleries and museums, but in the way we did as a child, from our own rich imaginations. We expressed from our inner selves because, like a child, it simply was so natural, felt so good, was so freeing, and seemed so necessary. We discovered our hearts had a lot to say.

Three years after I started the first class, during Thanksgiving break, a student said she "saw" me writing a book about the watercolor mandala classes. She said it would include both my mandalas and student's mandalas. "I can see it," she said. "It's a very simple, beautiful book." She looked at me suspecting I might not believe her and said, "I don't know what you think you ought to be doing, but I think you're supposed to be doing a book. Now!"

The truth was I had gotten the same inspiration. And so, the following year, I began to compile my mandalas and the mandalas from class participants for the book. I chose examples of work which I felt would demonstrate how the class was taught, how the process worked and how all of it evolved.

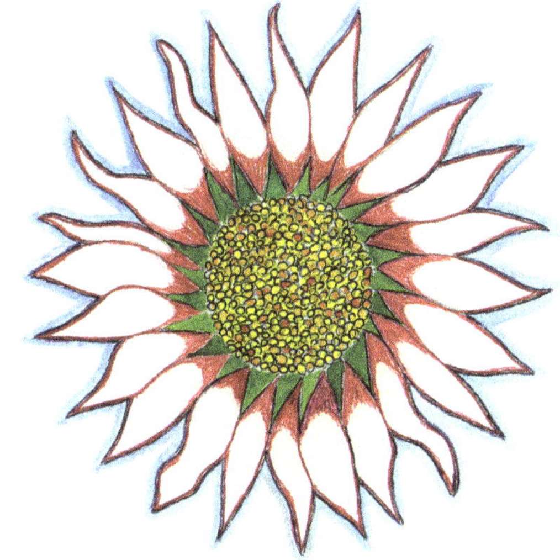

Lane Cara Shaw, *My First Mandala*, watercolor, colored pencil

"My life took on a new dimension when I went to Michele's 'Painting From the Heart' class, and began to draw my first mandala. I was well into my 'eighties' yet I sensed adventure! Our assignment was to think of ourselves as looking down on a flower, and to write what our intention was. Without hesitation I wrote, 'I want to know myself.' We were instructed to draw what we 'saw,' 'felt' or 'knew.' I knew I was to draw a bunch of seeds! That was within my range of capabilities, but my unexpected joy was my hand seemed to know where to go— it had a life of its own! I simply did my best to make all those seeds a little different. That was all I accomplished that night. In the days that followed, I propped up my drawing and each day until it was finished I was guided what to do. First there were the petals, all different sizes, then the various colors followed until the mandala was finished. Only much later I realized my drawing represented not only me, but everyone of us—we all come from the same Source, yet we each have our own individuality. We are so much more than most of us can imagine!"

–Lane Cara Shaw

HOW THE BOOK IS LAID OUT

THE BOOK IS LAID OUT as I taught the 6-8 week class. A section is devoted to each 2-hour class. There is an additional section called "Express Your Feelings," which is primarily devoted to homework and work outside of class. I encourage this because I believe the more you practice, the quicker you will catch on to the process and have it work for you. Also within the second chapter is a meditation to help with letting go to the divine spirit within and allowing it to help with the co-creative process.

The inspiration for each chapter came to me initially as I taught myself, or should I say, was guided, as to how to proceed with creating mandalas. In my own process I learned ways to create mandalas simply, with ease and without struggle. I focused on the process rather than the end result and that helped me let go of my own self-judgment. The chapters are presented in the way I learned, so that the process itself teaches you and leads you to an inner knowledge of yourself and the mandala. Each chapter contains a how-to guide for creating that mandala. Examples of mandalas done from the classes are included in each section.

This book was written with the idea that anyone who participates chapter by chapter with the assignments and suggestions, can do mandalas on their own and begin a most wonderful journey of self-expression and self-discovery. No previous experience of art or painting is necessary at all. Really! Follow the suggestions. It is not a hard process, and it is enormously satisfying. All you need is the willingness to try, a few art materials, some time to yourself, and, most importantly, the suspension of self-judgment.

This is meaningful and fun inner work and is not intended to be done as "art work" to hang on your wall. Some of the work may, in fact, find its way to your walls, but the intention from the beginning is not that. It is for you to go inside yourself, and to see what comes out. To journey to and explore your inner world, the kingdom within, which is full of so many treasures. Remember, especially if you are new to any part of this process, you are a beginner. Honor that as you would if you were watching a child learn to walk or learn to paint. Give yourself space and time. Be gentle. No judgements. And, if you can do that, you're on your way. Your way, not anyone else's. Good luck and happy painting. Remember, have fun, what's the point otherwise? Entertain yourself, know yourself. You are the adventure. Enjoy the journey.

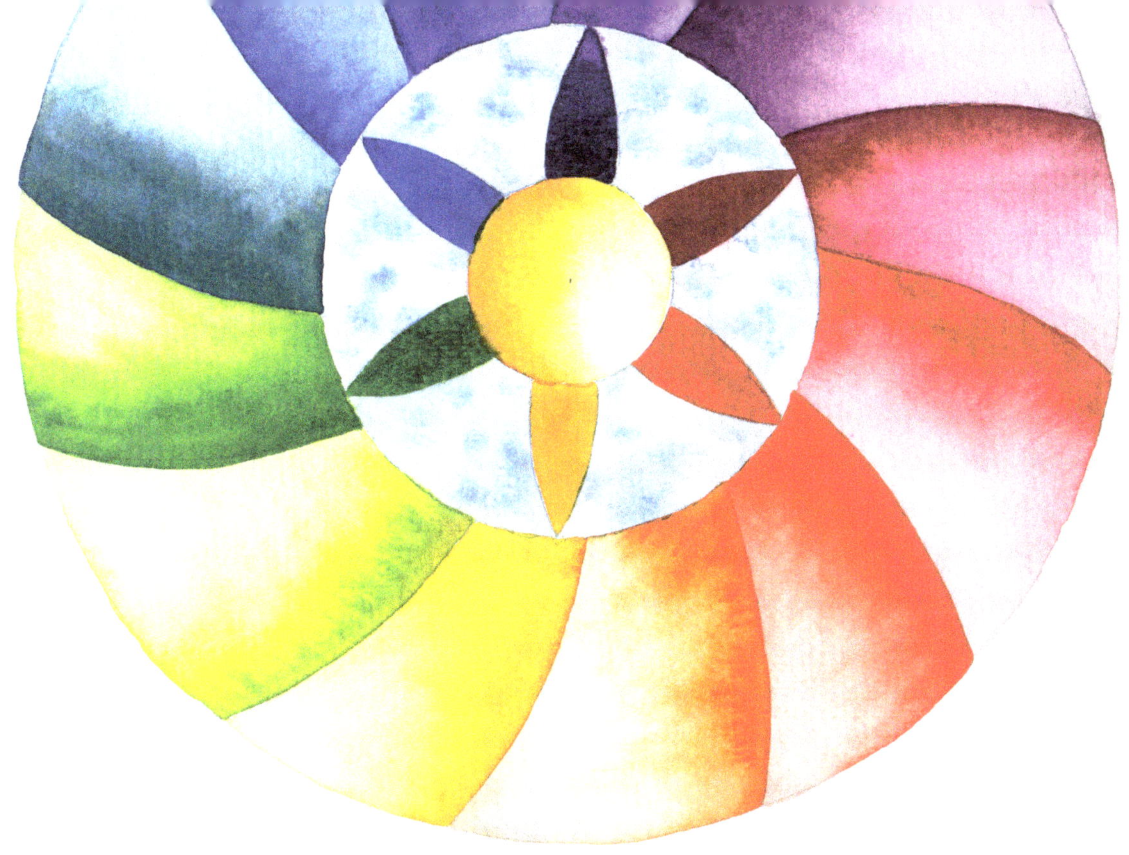

CHAPTER ONE

GETTING STARTED

GATHERING MATERIALS

Box of Watercolors

Now that you're ready to begin, the first thing you will need is your art supplies. A Suggested Material's List is included at the end of this chapter. Look it over before you go to the art store. See what you may already have or can substitute. If you determine this ahead of time, and know exactly what you want to buy, you won't make the mistake of just handing the list to the salesperson and ending up with either a very big bill or things you may not need immediately. When you do start purchasing your supplies, buy the best that you can afford within your budget. Don't get carried away buying all kinds of fancy equipment and supplies, it isn't necessary. Do what you can in order to get started. That's the important thing. Improvise if you have to. That's why some people choose to begin with a ready-made inexpensive palette of cake watercolors. They find it less intimidating and using these palettes reminds them of painting as a child. If you would prefer to do that, just to give this process a try before you invest in a lot of supplies, I would recommend a small box of Prang Watercolors. It comes with an inexpensive brush which you could use temporarily, but only temporarily, because a good brush is essential. If you do choose the cake color palette, then for now, you can skip to the paragraph on watercolor paper.

Watercolor Pigments

Buy the best quality watercolor pigments you can afford. Once you've graduated from the watercolor cakes, pigments in tubes are preferred and they come in student grade and artist grade quality, the student grade being much less expensive. I started with student grade and eventually moved to artist grade and use several different brands depending on the colors. Student grade is very good paint to begin with. Remember, tube colors can last a long time and go a long way as you only use a little bit each session. Choose the basic colors you like, and add more later when you wish to expand your color palette.

Check the permanence rating on the tubes and get the ones with the best ratings, so the colors won't fade. Shopping for new colors is fun, especially real bright colors, which, when mixed with other colors, can give you interesting variations and really make the colors snap. I use black and white very sparingly. I use white to make a pastel shade, but I never paint with white straight from the tube. Rarely will I use black straight from the tube, and then only a small bit to "gray" a color.

Choose colors you like. I rarely pick a color I don't like to paint with because I am very careful to get shades which resonate with me. There are lots and lots of shades of every color. Find the ones you like, ones that make you excited about painting. One student came to class with colors she had hurriedly picked up the night before. But when she got to class and began painting with them, she couldn't stand the shades she had picked. That made it hard for her to enjoy painting. It taught me a lesson, too. Buy colors which express who you are!

Watercolor Palette

If you use tube pigments you'll need a palette for the paint. I use a small, portable, rectangular, plastic white palette with plenty of small wells for pigment and bigger spaces for mixing. It has a hinged lid so that I can close it and carry it to class in my art box. You will be squeezing the tube paint into the small wells. After your painting session don't wash away this pigment, allow it to dry and save it for the next session. The dry paint is activated by simply adding a drop or two of water to it. The palette should also have larger spaces for mixing colors, and these spaces *are* cleaned up after your painting session.

Brushes

Just to get started you can begin with only one brush, the size 6 round. When you find you need a smaller brush for details, get a size 2 round. For bigger washes add a size 12 round. A good, sturdy synthetic brush for beginners is the Winsor Newton Series 233. I have used these brushes myself as I find I wear out expensive natural brushes too quickly in this particular kind of work. Don't skimp on brushes. A good brush is vital. Make sure the brush is called a watercolor brush, has a short handle and the bristles come to a point when wet (try it out with water in the store.) Good brushes will have a seamless ferrel (the part that holds the bristles.) Take good care of your brushes so they will last. *Don't leave them sitting in water.* Wash them after each session with a little mild soap and water. When you store them, bring the bristles to a point to dry, so they won't bend.

Watercolor Paper

Good paper is also essential. Don't skimp here either. The Strathmore 300 or 400 Series, 11"x15," is the best inexpensive pad I've found. I don't recommend any lighter weight paper than this 130 or 140 lb as it wrinkles and buckles too much. When I paint larger mandalas than this size, I buy large sheets of Arches watercolor paper, either cold pressed or hot pressed (smooth), and cut them down to the size I want. (Many of my mandalas are 15"x15".) But, I have used lots of the Strathmore 140 lb watercolor pads, painting with the paper removed from the pad. (Gummed binding is easier to remove from the pad than wire binding.) There is one exception to this. When on a trip or vacation I take along a smaller wire-bound 9"x12" Strathmore watercolor pad. I leave the paper in the pad (which creates a hard surface for me to work on) and paint smaller mandalas. These have become journals of the inner experiences of my travels and a way to bring the energy home.

Other Supplies

The other supplies are self-explanatory. You will want a hard enough pencil so that if you draw, the lines are light enough to erase, should you make a "mistake," and also light enough not to show too much under the watercolor washes. The Magic Rub eraser is great for that and does not damage the watercolor paper if erasing is done lightly. The gold and silver inks or felt pens are fun to have to play with, and everyone seems to love using the gold ink in their mandalas. Add other supplies you find interesting and fun.

THE WATERCOLOR WASHES

Let's get started by practicing four basic watercolor washes. And the important word here is PRACTICE. We are only playing and practicing right now. Get out all of your supplies. Fill your water jar with clean water. Grab a couple of paper towels. Lay out a sheet of watercolor paper—if it's in a pad, tear it out. Activate your dry watercolors by adding a drop or two of water to each color. If you are using tube watercolors, squeeze out a blob of paint of each color into your small palette wells. I start with white at one end, black at the other and graduate the colors in between from light to dark. Draw a circle in the center of your paper with your compass. (We'll use this circle after we practice the washes.) We will be practicing the four washes around the circle, one along each side of the paper, so give yourself enough room outside of the circle. See the *Diagram of Four Watercolor Washes* below which shows examples of the four basic washes.

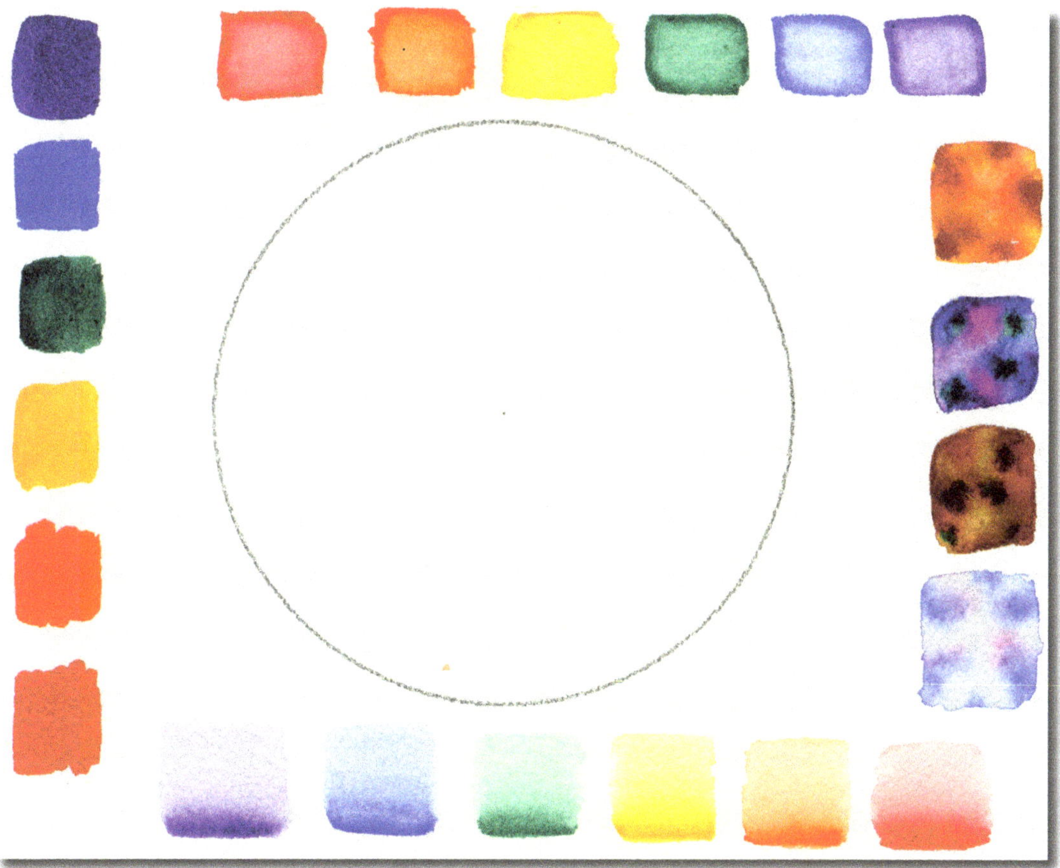

Diagram of Four Watercolor Washes (clockwise from the top): Lift, Irregular, Gradated, and Flat

Flat Wash

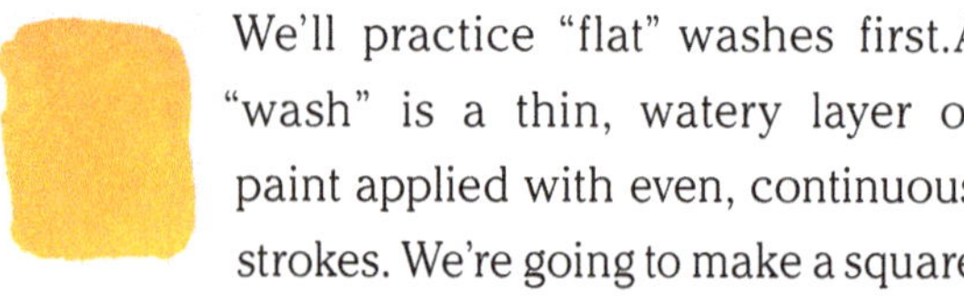

We'll practice "flat" washes first. A "wash" is a thin, watery layer of paint applied with even, continuous strokes. We're going to make a square practice wash of each color across the top of your paper. I usually start with red and paint colors in the order they appear in a rainbow. Dampen your brush in the water, and lift a bit of red pigment from the paint well to a mixing space. Add a little bit of water and mix the paint and water until you have a nice even mix of red pigment and water—neither too thick nor thin. This will take time and practice for you to get the feel of this.

At the top left of the paper make a square about an inch wide or so, by moving the brush at an angle horizontally back and forth continuously until it makes a smooth, even square wash. See the diagram on the previous page. The idea is to get a flat, even surface. The more you go over it, the more unwanted streaks and spots will occur. Remember this is a practice. Streaks and spots are normal for watercolor, so don't panic if they happen. So, now practice a square wash with each of your other five basic colors—orange, yellow, green, blue and violet. If you want to be more creative with this, make other shapes, and use other colors. There are no rules here, so just go ahead, get started and have fun. Wash your brush out in your water jar after each color you use. When your water turns brown get clean water! Clean water is essential.

Lift

Let's practice the "lift" technique with a row of squares along a different side of your paper. Rotate your paper so you are working along the top. In the *Diagram of Four Watercolor Washes* the lift squares are along the top side of the paper. Start by making a flat wash as you did with the previous wash. This time, however, after making the wash, immediately rinse the color from your brush in your jar of water, leaving your brush with a small amount of water in it. In the middle of the flat wash which you just laid down, drop the water from your brush. Now dry your brush by dabbing it on a piece of paper towel. Go back and lift the color out of the middle of the flat wash where you dropped the water with your brush. Pick up the watery paint with the brush and wipe the brush on the paper towel. Do this over and over until you've lifted the color out of the middle of the square. It will be lighter than the surrounding darker color. If you wanted to do this even more quickly, dab the middle of your flat wash square lightly with a soft tissue. This should lift the color out immediately. What you have created with a lift is the effect of light coming through your square. Practice with all your colors as shown.

Gradated Wash

Rotate your paper again so that you are working along the top side. With a clean brush full of a little water, let's practice the "gradated wash." In the diagram this wash is along the bottom of the paper. In this row of washes, paint a square that is just clear water, but not too much water. Then, get some color in your brush and drag the brush along the top of the wet square in a line. Quickly wash the pigment out your brush. With a clean and slightly damp brush, touch the edge of the stroke you've just made and draw the color down the wet surface by moving the brush back and forth horizontally across the wet square. What you should have is an area of color which graduates or "gradates" from dark to light, from top to bottom. This takes a lot of practice and "feel" for how much water and pigment to use. Be patient with yourself. Practice with your other colors. This wash is called a "wet-on-wet" gradated wash because you wet your paper first. It can also be done on dry paper. Try it by applying a line of color along the top of a dry square. Wash the pigment from your brush. Now drag down, or stroke back and forth, a wash of color by touching the edge of the stroke you just applied, with your clean, damp brush. Use whichever wash works best for you. I'm a big fan of wet-on-wet washes, they just work best for me.

Irregular Wash

Again, turn your paper so you are working along the top side. On the fourth side of your paper, let's try my favorite, the "irregular" wash. This is also a wet-on-wet technique. Start as you did with the wet-on-wet gradated wash, by making a square wet wash with no pigment. While the square is still wet, drop any color of pigment on it with your brush, wherever you wish, and let the color run or flow randomly. Rinse the first color out of your brush and get a different color on your brush. Dot that color on another area of the wet square, letting that color run or "bleed" into the first color. Dot another color or colors into the square if you want. Try picking your paper up and tilting it so the colors run together. Or, drip a small drop of clear water onto the square making the colors run, bleed or "puddle" even more. I can sit and play with wet-on-wet areas in my paintings almost endlessly, adding more pigment, then water, then lifting out color in other areas, and repeating it all again. It is delicate though, and you have to learn to get a feel for how much, or how little, water and pigment to use. Don't "scrub" on it, or you'll have a mess. Although, "messes" are a good way to learn and experiment, so drip away. There are no mistakes. If you add too many colors together you will get brown, and it can look muddy. That seems to be a common fear. Notice what gives you mud, and then use it when you need mud! Otherwise, use less water and less pigment and see what happens. Experiment and watch how the watercolor will stay within the wet square you made–the watercolor will only go into the wet areas.

Sky Effects (Wet-on-Wet Irregular Wash)

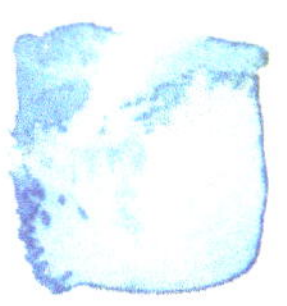

I use a wet-on-wet, irregular wash technique for the sky-like effects I frequently use in my work. First, I mix up a good amount of sky blue in a big mixing space. This I do by adding a dot or two of blue *to* the several drops of white, mixing it together and diluting it with a bit of water. I check to see that I have mixed enough color to adequately cover the area I'm going to paint. Next, I wet the entire area I want to paint sky blue. I then randomly drop the sky blue color I've mixed on the wet surface. I play with it by adding drops of clear water to some white areas to make "clouds" and lifting color out of other areas. This is the only way you can get white in transparent watercolor, by letting the white of the paper show through. I then add more of the sky blue mixture to yet other areas. I repeat this over and over until I get the desired effect of interesting patterns of sky (the sky blue color I mixed) and clouds (the white of the paper.) This is really fun. I have spent many hours creating skies. This is like a meditation for me.

SUGGESTED MATERIALS LIST

Watercolor Brushes
Simply Simmons or equivalent:
Size 6 round, short handle
Size 2 round, short handle (optional)
Size 12 round, short handle (optional)

Pigments
Student grade small tubes of these colors:

red	*blue*
orange	*violet*
yellow	*black*
green	*white*

Watercolor Paper
Strathmore 300 or 400 Series
12" square or 11" x 15" pad,
130 lb. or 140 lb. cold pressed or rough

Other Supplies
Palette with wells for pigment (spaces for mixing)
and portable (with a lid)
Jar for water
Pencil (no. 2 or harder)
Eraser: Magic Rub
Compass (I use an Alvin 702V)
Ruler
Paper towels
Tissue

Optional
Jars of Winsor Newton gold or
silver water soluble inks
Pilot gold and silver marker pens, ex. fine pt.
Art box or tool box to carry your supplies
Portfolio to keep your work in

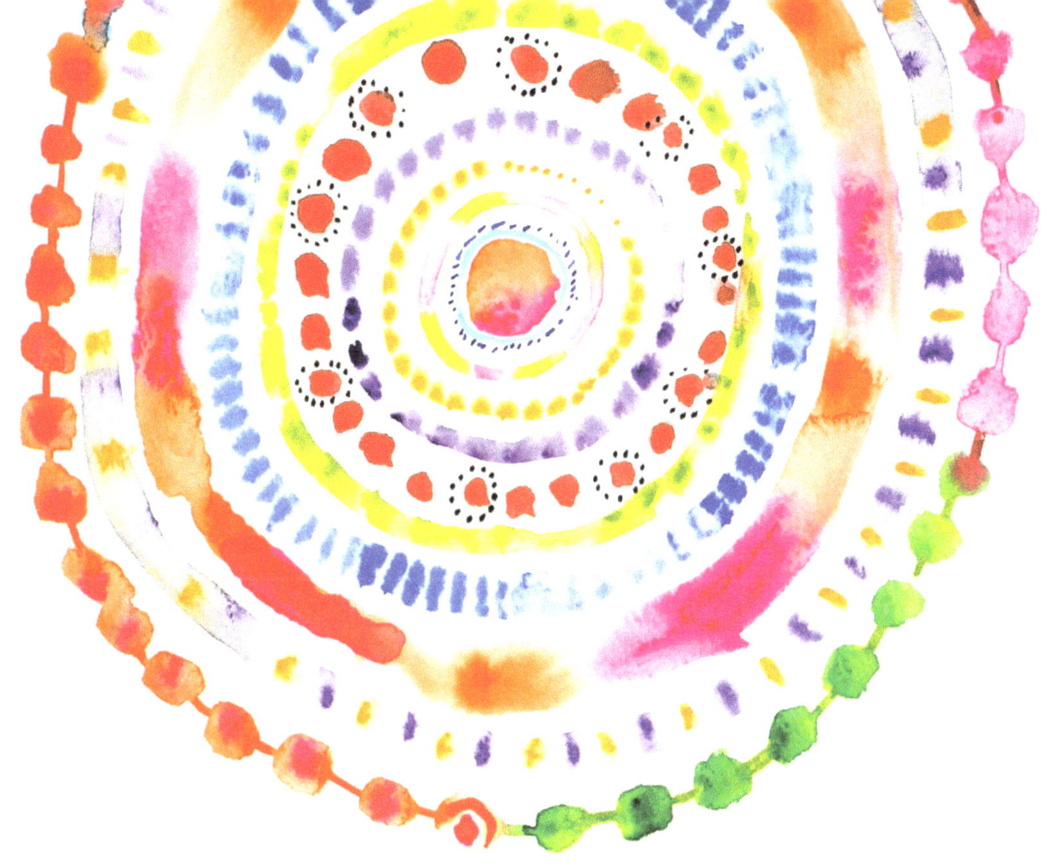

CHAPTER TWO

Creating A Quick Mandala

A Place To Get Started

The idea of a quick mandala, or "quickie man-dala" as I often call it, came about when I was asked to put together a 2-hour mandala painting class for a group who were attending a week-long Elderhostel Program. It was to be held at a local Buddhist retreat center called "A Place to Develop a Good Heart." I was a little worried, wondering if they would understand in such a limited amount of time. When the group filed in that evening af-ter a big hike, looking worn from their full day of activities, I did get nervous with their protests of "I can't" and "I'm too tired." I showed them the ba-sic watercolor washes, did a meditation and gave them this mandala exercise. By the end, we had a class of energized folks, many of whom were "amazed" that they were enjoying painting for the first time since they were children.

A quick mandala is just as it sounds. It's place to get started. It's quick, it's fast. Many people have not done any painting since grammar school and sometimes find it hard to get started. They are afraid of making a mess, afraid their watercolors will become muddy or afraid that what they do will not be "art." These quick mandalas allow us to begin where we left off as children, beginners playing, exploring and inventing. Little children for the most part don't have hang-ups about what their art looks like. They have such wonderful, free energy and it comes out in their work. We like looking at children's art for this reason. It's so energetic and creative, because they just go for it. The energy and magic come through. And, believe me, you have the same. As you paint, let a part of you be the "observer," unattached to the outcome and simply watch the magic unfold.

TRUTH AND CREATIVITY

Most people are very surprised at what occurs when painting a quick mandala. Old, static energy begins to move. It can be a very powerful experience. The excitement of your own creative energy and movement from within brings new life into the nooks and crannies you've forgotten are there. "So the sages say, if you pause and feel the truth of your own heart, everything is transformed for you."[1]

Julia Cameron says in *The Artist's Way* that in the truth is where true creativity lies, and from my own experience, I completely agree. You simply can't "try" to be creative. Creativity comes from expressing who and where you are—telling the truth in your heart.

"But it's muck," said one student. Then paint the muck, because if you don't it will stay there until you acknowledge it. Muck is a great cesspool of energy. When you do honor it, or "own" it by painting it, the muck has a way of releasing great stored reserves and transforms into something else. Isn't that the benefit of a great compost pile? And, it is your very own!

PAINTING FROM THE CENTER

I usually paint from the center of the paper outward, concentrically and somewhat symmetrically, around the center as I focus and "concentrate" on my own, inner center. When I first began painting mandalas I did not want to be confined by a circle, so I did not draw a circle first and work within it. A great example of that is in Karlene Koketsu's *Quickie Mandala*. Another example of working in that way is in *Campo Dei Fiori* by Don Faia, my husband. I now work both ways, sometimes within a pre-drawn circle and sometimes without. I'll elaborate more on that in later chapters and in other mandalas.

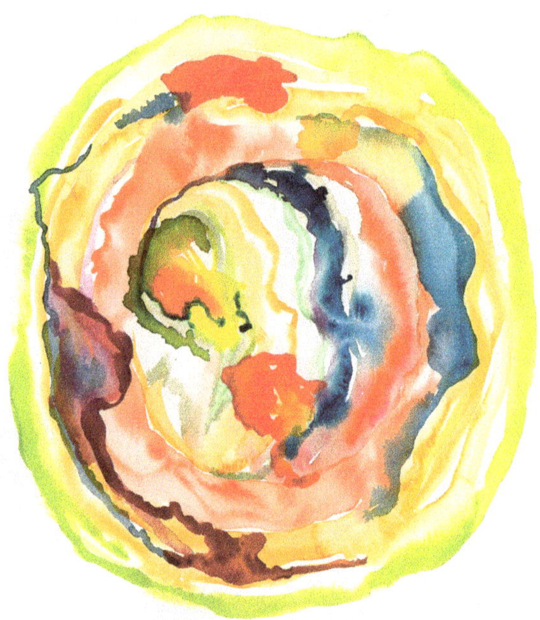

Karlene Koketsu, *Quickie Mandala*, watercolor

Karlene did not work within a pre-drawn circle in this mandala. She started in the middle of her paper and worked outward, keeping the mandala circular in shape as it unfolded.

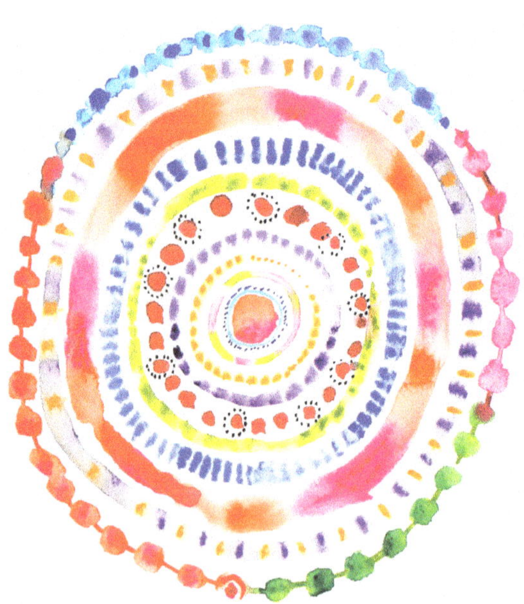

Don Faia, *Campo Dei Fiori (Field of Flowers,)* watercolor

This mandala was done by painting concentric rings of various watercolor techniques. This is a simple, fun and fast way to paint a quick mandala.

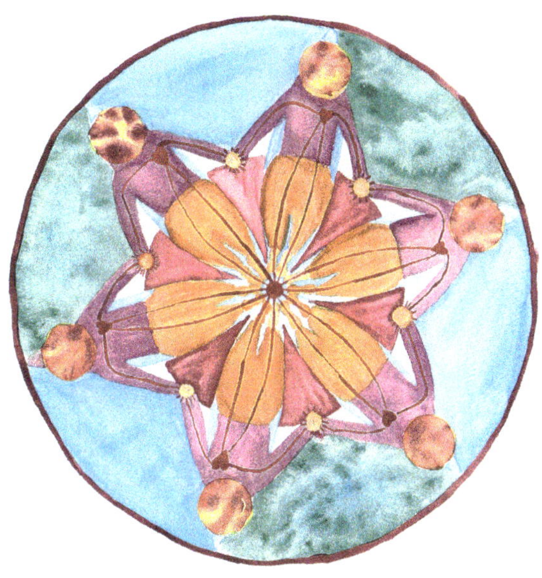

April Hyder, *The Fire of Meditation*, watercolor

Meditating with others in a group, all of whom are holding
the same intention, can generate a powerful spiritual
energy which is healing in itself. April Hyder shows
us her experience of the Grounding Meditation.

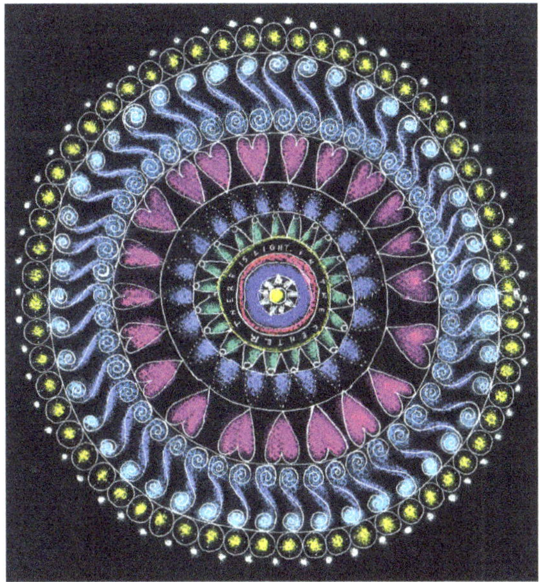

Don Faia, *In The Center There is Light*, white ink, pastel

Don did not believe he could "see" images in meditation.
I suggested he try meditating in class with an intention
and chanting. When I saw the look on his face after the
meditation, I knew he had been successful. This mandala
is what he "saw." He liked using black paper and white
ink and experimenting with other different materials.

MEDITATING AND MANDALAS

An essential part of the mandala process is meditation. For those not familiar with meditation, it is practiced primarily to quiet our minds, freeing us from our internal mind chatter. It is a way of becoming conscious of consciousness. It has been described as inward prayer, or listening, rather than talking to God or the All-That-Is. "The purpose of meditation is to attain divine grace.... The secret of grace is contact with the Infinite Invisible, the universal center of being within us... this spiritual experience is called Illumination, Cosmic Consciousness or Christ-Consciousness; in the New Testament, it is spoken of as being 'born again,' or 'rebirth.'"[2] When we meditate we can come into the flow of the creative energy of the universe and feel peaceful, and renewed.

I have included the guided meditation that I use in class at the end of this chapter. It is called a "Grounding Meditation," and is actually guided imagery in which we use the earth's energy to ground, calm and energize us. (See April Hyder's mandala.) Taught to me by a Reiki master, energetic healer and teacher, I have used it for years and find it a wonderful tool for everyone. The teacher told me that earth energy is the easiest energy for us to bring into our bodies and it will nourish us deeply. You can use this meditation, or one of your own.

Another more simple form of meditation is to sit quietly with your eyes closed and become aware of, or "watch," your breath. Try breathing in deep and breathing out long. As thoughts arise let them pass by like clouds in the sky. Some people take a seed thought or phrase into meditation and say it inwardly as they breathe. This concentration on a thought, or the breath, called concentration meditation, helps focus and calm the mind.

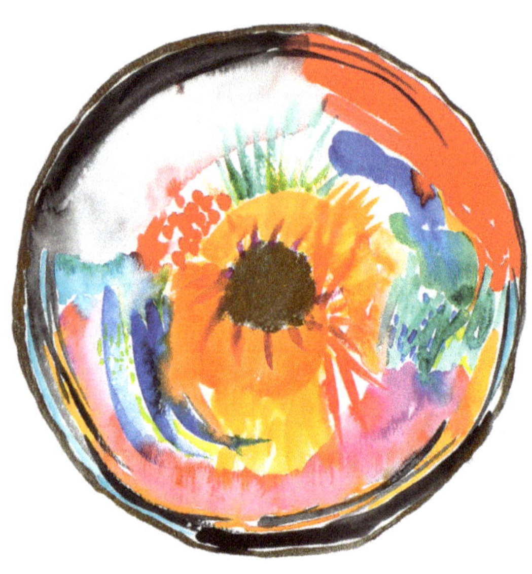

Quickie Mandala, watercolor, gold ink

In this mandala I let myself experiment with techniques
and color, painting freely however I wanted. It is bold and
spontaneous and I had no worries about how
it was going to turn out.

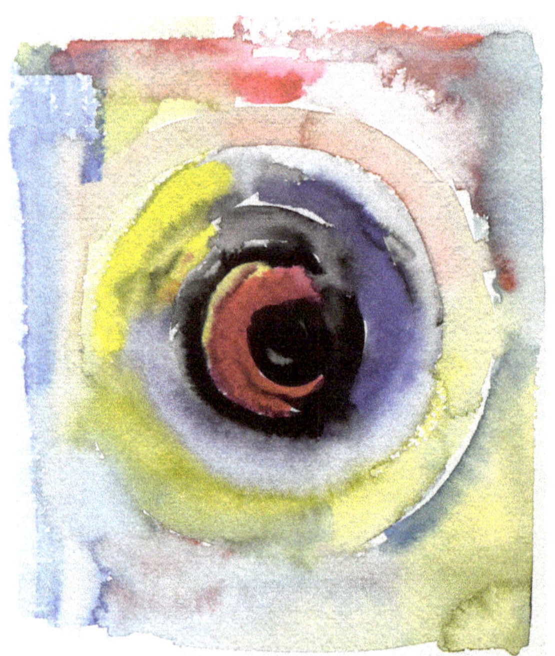

Sara Fisher-Smith, *Colors of Spring,* watercolor

Against her will/Her child's heart
Calls forth
Colors of Spring/And Laughs
—Sara Fisher-Smith

CHANTING

While leading the class meditation I usually play "The Eternal Om" by *Valley of the Sun* as background music. OM is the oldest sound of the universe and is said to be the sound of creation. It is also very similar to the sound of Amen. It is extremely helpful to chant OM in a group or alone as a way to invoke creation, and it really does work. We did not chant in class for the first couple of years of the mandala work, but I kept getting the message that we should. Once we began there was a real difference in the mandalas. They were richer, deeper and flowed more easily. Chanting with a group, of course, is a powerful and centering experience, but I sometimes chant at home alone before I do a mandala, under my breath, keeping to myself. That works very well for me. We have been given access to so many helpful tools, why not use them all? Reciting a favorite prayer is also a wonderful way to invoke the creative spirit.

How To Get Started On The Quick Mandala

THE QUICK MANDALA is a great way to get started, so let's begin before you think too hard about it. We're ready to use the circle in the middle of the paper which you drew earlier (in Chapter One) and which is now surrounded by your practice washes. (If they are still wet, you can give them a quick drying with a hair dryer.) Or, if you wish, take a fresh sheet of paper and draw a large circle in the middle of it with your compass. On the back of your paper write your intention for this exercise; expressing your intention helps you focus clearly on what you wish to have happen, both during your meditation, and your painting. For example, my suggestion for this mandala's intention would be: "Playing in a quickie mandala." The idea in this exercise is for you to get started quickly, have fun and play, and to be present in your truth.

Another way to state your intention would be to write "painting the now," or "painting the truth in my heart." The circle we have circumscribed really represents the now, not the past, not the future, but the present time. It is your sacred space. You may want to write the intention in your own words. If you do, always follow what is your truth, at this moment. Never jump ahead of where you are or how you are feeling. One student asked, "Do I write your intention?" Only if it is true for you now. Otherwise, write your own intention. If you sit down to paint the mandala in this exercise, or any of the exercises, and something else inside is calling to you, rather than the suggested intention, then you must follow that, and write your intention accordingly.

Next put on some playful, easy, instrumental music and sit in a relaxed, but erect position. Close your eyes, breathe deeply, and relax. You may want to use the meditation I use in class, which is included at the end of this chapter. Draw your attention inward. Notice how you feel, right now in this moment. What is going on in the center of yourself, in your heart? What is your truth, right now? Become aware of that. Imagine bringing your intention, which you wrote on your paper, into your heart. What colors and shapes are your feelings?

When you get a good sense of what's in your center, in your heart, when you feel you are in touch with it, gently open your eyes, pick up your brush and begin to paint what you feel, inside the circle. Move to the music. What color do you feel you want to use first, and second, and so on? Let the brush go wherever it wants and make whatever marks it wants to make. Use the washes you've just learned, or don't, as you wish. Paint from the inside out, not with your mind, but from the inside of your being. Whatever you like, whatever you feel, explore like a child, trying, experimenting, dabbing, stroking, with big lines or little dots, with wet washes or dry strokes. That is how I created the 1996 *Quickie Mandala*. Let yourself be surprised, let go and let it happen. No judgements, just flow with the energy. Because you are, in a sense, painting energy, the energy will come down your arm and hand and almost paint itself. Don't hold it back, let it come through your hand. Remember, have fun, that's the point!

After the wet paint in your mandala has dried, turn your paper over and on the backside date your work, give it a title if you'd like and make any notes about your process which you may want to remember later. I have been so glad I've done that, when years later, I'll read what I wrote and see that it is still relevant. Sometimes the writing will come in the form of a poem as in Sara Fishersmith's *Colors of Spring*. Finally, hang up your mandala in a safe place, away from judgemental eyes. It will teach you about yourself if you let it. Once again, it is for teaching, not judging yourself!

GROUNDING MEDITATION

GENTLY CLOSE YOUR EYES. Place your feet flat on the floor. Sit up straight in your chair with your spine erect. Take in three deep breaths slowly and let out the cares of the day. Bring your attention now to your two feet on the floor, and begin to imagine them stretching and growing through the floor, through the foundation of the building and into the earth below. With each breath you take, you become more and more relaxed, and your feet grow further into the earth. The earth welcomes your feet! Allow your feet to gently grow, deeper and deeper into the earth. Hundreds and hundreds of miles your feet flow down into the earth. Deeper and deeper into the ground. Deeper and deeper down. Your feet are now thousands of miles down into the earth. Eventually, your feet come to the center of the earth, the heart of mother earth, where you find a most magnificent energy, the creative energy of the earth, the creative energy of the universe. It is a beautiful, glowing gold light. Allow your feet to comfortably, gently, safely touch down into this energy. Begin to imagine this energy, this gold light, flowing into your feet and allow it to flow up into your stretched legs. Just allow, don't push, this beautiful energy up your stretched feet and legs. Allow the gold light to flow, gently, easily back up your feet and legs. Stay connected to that energy flowing up from the center of the earth. Allow that gold light to travel all the way back up to the surface of the earth, through the foundation of the building and into your feet on the floor. Feel the gold light now enter your legs, your torso and flow throughout your body. Fill your body with the energy from the center of the earth. Take a moment now to double the energy coming from the center of the earth. Double it again, so that you are in a virtual river of gold light and energy, in and around your body. Allow the energy to meet your own light inside yourself. The energies combine and you become a mass of light and energy. Now bring this energy down your arms and your hands and charge your paper and your tools with this energy. Bring the energy into your heart chamber and fill it with gold light and energy. Bring your intention from the back of your paper into your heart. Charge your intention with more energy by doing the OM Chant 4 times:

OMMMMM. OMMMMM. OMMMMM. OMMMMM.

Sit quietly in the silence and gently begin to notice what you have received from your intention. It may be a vision, or a feeling, or a thought, or a knowing. Perhaps you may think you have received nothing. Whatever you received, and however you received it, is exactly perfect for you right now. Give thanks for what you received.

When you are ready, gently bring yourself back into the room, and gently open your eyes. Hold the silence so you can stay centered as you do your work. Remember to remain connected to the gold light and allow it to help you create your mandala. Trust, and let go.

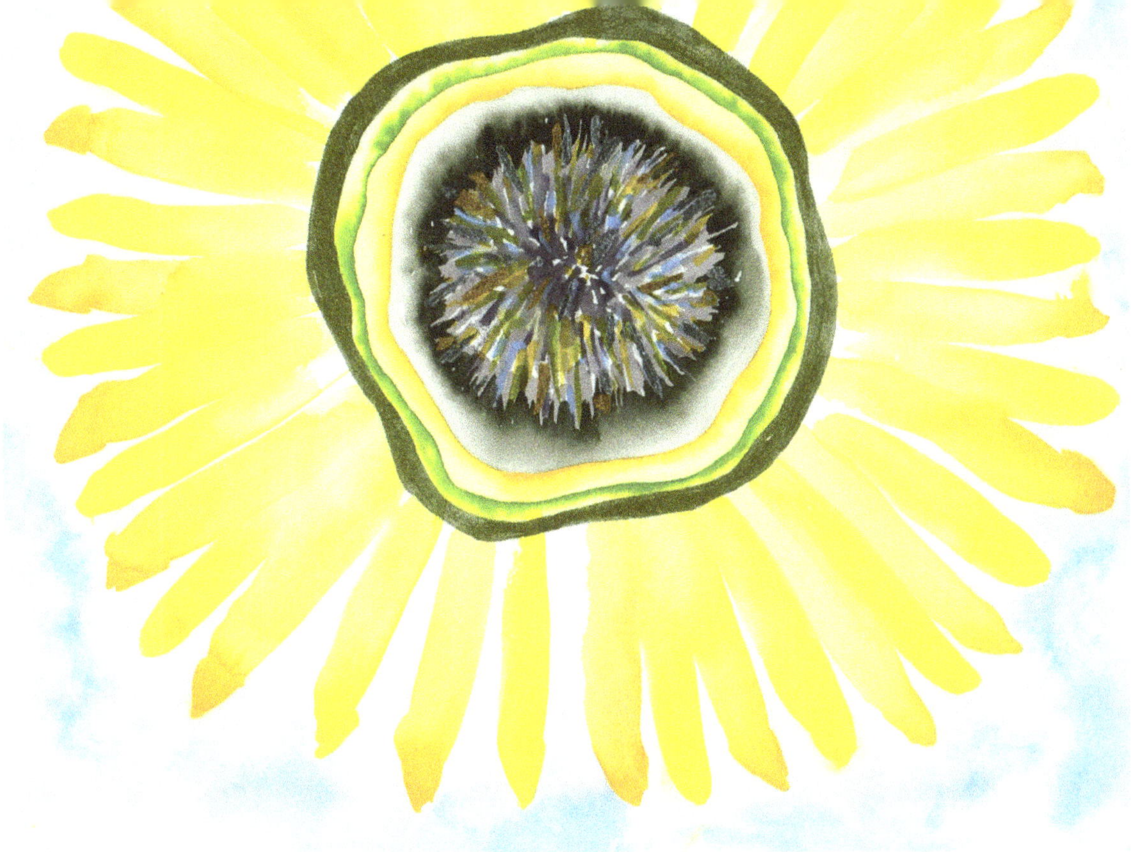

CHAPTER THREE

Express Your Feelings

A Way To Practice Quick Mandalas

"I was painting to have a dialogue with myself."
–Jess

Having now tried mandalas, I suggest taking the opportunity to practice the quick mandala process. This is the chapter I call "homework." And, there is no richer place to start than at home, that is, with your own feelings.

Mandalas begin with a turning within oneself, and are truly a journey to our own center. Different from our outer-directed daily life, mandalas provide a path for what really is a personal pilgrimage. Carl Jung, the well-known Swiss psychiatrist who brought the awareness of mandalas into the 20th century, once said that "the only real adventure remaining for each individual was the exploration of one's own Self;" the ultimate goal being to form a harmonious and balanced relationship with it.[1]

Painting Emotions In Mandalas

The importance and focus of our mandala work is not so much the end product, or the result of what we have done. It is more about the process, being on an inward, focused path and opening up to what is happening on our journey. When we are on a spiritual path to our inner life, we will encounter many emotions along the way. Painting emotions in mandalas can be transformational. Emotions can be processed this way, and, I, as well as many others, have found that mandalas bring clarity, insight and balance to the emotional self. In his autobiography, Carl Jung writes about his experience with mandalas during a very "ominous" time:

"It was only toward the end of the First World War that I gradually began to emerge from the darkness.... I sketched every morning in a notebook a small circular drawing, a mandala, which seemed to correspond to my inner situation at

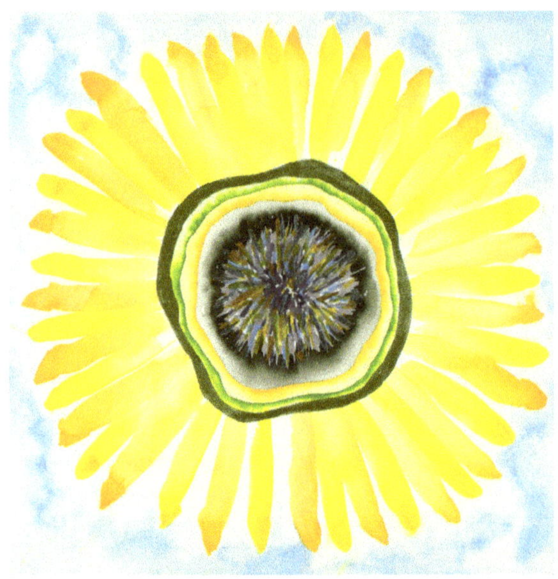

The Possibility of Happiness, watercolor, foil

I awoke from a dream with an image of a sunflower on my chest and feelings of the possibility of happiness. I felt so good, and by painting the mandala I could deepen my experience and linger in the good feelings.

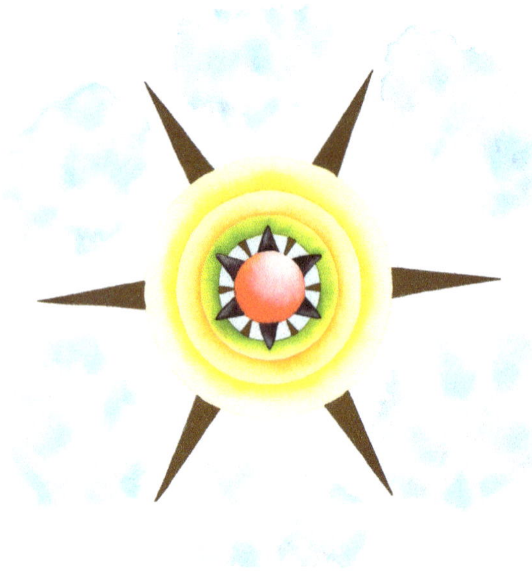

The Hidden Boil, watercolor, gold felt pen

To my surprise I kind of liked this mandala when I finished it. It wasn't as ugly or as angry looking as I had felt. Also, because I didn't know what the mandala was going to look like prior to finishing it, my inner critic was more curious than judgmental and suspended criticism. That is often the case for me in mandala painting.

the time. With the help of these drawings I could observe my psychic transformations from day to day.... My mandalas were cryptograms concerning the state of the self which were presented to me anew each day.... To be sure, at first I could only dimly understand them, and I guarded them like precious pearls.... During those years, between 1918 and 1920, I began to understand that the goal of psychic development is the self... everything points toward the center. This insight gave me stability, and gradually my inner peace returned. I knew that in finding the mandala as an expression of the self I had attained what was for me the ultimate. Perhaps someone else knows more, but not I."[2]

BALANCING AN EMOTION

When you are in the middle of feeling an emotion you would like to balance, try painting a mandala using the process described for the quick mandala in the previous chapter. *Colors of Spring*, in Chapter 2, is an example of how one student did it. When I do this kind of a mandala, I generally start small and work quickly. My intention is to spend just a few minutes processing and painting the emotions, that way I know I'll be more likely to actually sit down and do it!

Sometimes however, I will spend more time than a few minutes on emotions in a mandala because it feels so good to process through them. I like coming through the feelings, lighter, more clear and balanced. This is just what happened in *The Possibility of Happiness* in which I moved through fear and into happiness, or sunshine. Note what Jung said about expressing emotions through imagery: "To the extent that I managed to translate the emotions into images—that is to say, to find images which were concealed in the emotions—I was inwardly calmed and reassured. Had I left those images hidden in the emotions, I might have been torn to pieces by them."[3]

I had an interesting experience of this in my early mandala work. I had become very frustrated with one of my health practitioners, wanting more answers and help than she was able to give. Feeling like I was going to boil over, and fearing I would explode, I "sat" on those feelings and consequently developed a boil on my back side. I decided to paint a mandala to relieve the emotional pressure. In *The Hidden Boil* I started with a red dot or hot spot in the middle of my paper, putting all the frustration I felt into it, and worked in concentric rings, outward from the center. I really calmed down and felt peaceful by the end of the painting, which took about an hour. The next day the boil vanished, leaving me a little awestruck by the power of the process.

THIS IS A GREAT TOOL

This is a great tool. Not only can you paint feelings which you are processing and balancing, but those which you wish to dive into more deeply—joy, happiness, gratitude, bliss. With these feelings, I find the mandalas can get more involved than what the perimeters of the quick mandala provide. We'll do those next.

Enjoy the process, let go of the end result and enjoy your emotions as Carol-lyn Davis did in her mandala *My Emotions Add Color And Depth To My Life*. You can have a lot of fun painting all kinds of feelings, even the jitters from coffee, as in Marilyn Lucier's *Coffee Jangled Nerves*. Just remember that emotions provide very good fuel for your journey!

Mandalas have been a wonderful, healthy and safe place for me to express emotions which I am in the process of assimilating. I now have a place to work with these feelings and can stop stuffing them away in my body, which has caused me an array of health issues. In the mandala process, we can unravel a lot of buried "stuff" as in Phyllis Hill's dramatic *Unfolding*.

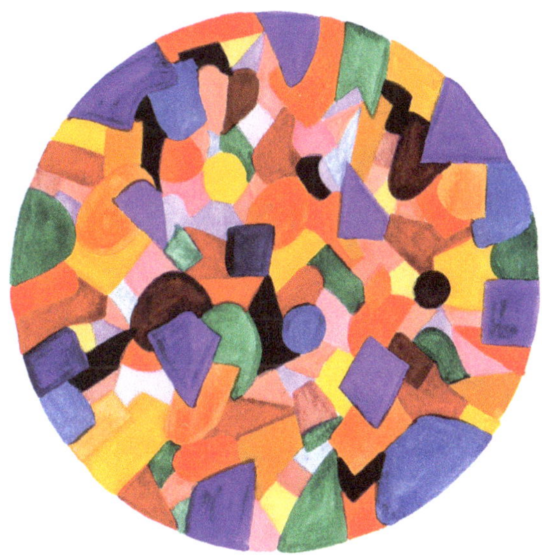

Carol-lyn Davis, *My Emotions Add Color and Depth To My Life*, watercolor pens

Carol-lyn liked expressing her feelings in mandalas and she painted lots of them. She shared them in class which helped everyone become more comfortable with the process.

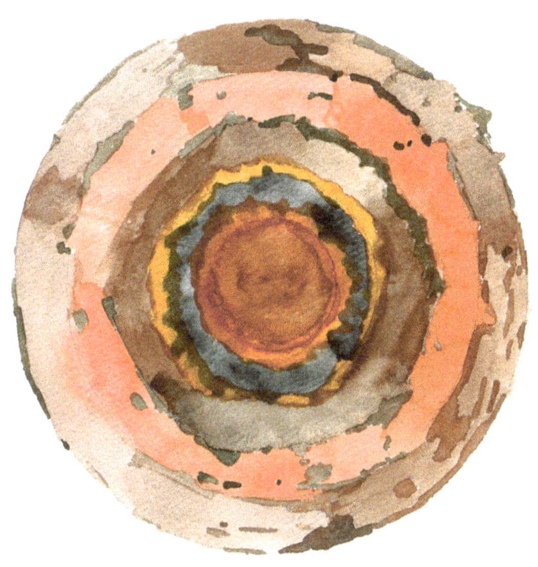

Marilyn Lucier, *Coffee Jangled Nerves*, watercolor

It was fascinating to watch what Marilyn would choose to paint in her mandalas and what beautiful and unique colors she would create.

EXPRESSING YOUR FEELINGS IN A MANDALA

START BY WRITING your intention on the back of your piece of watercolor paper. If it will help you begin, start small, even on a piece of scrap paper, and don't worry or think about the outcome. Your intention can be just one word—anxiety, anger, loneliness, joy, gratitude, etc. You can be more elaborate, but I often will write just one word for these emotion mandalas. Draw a circle on the front of your paper. Go into yourself, your center, into the feelings, and begin to paint what the feeling feels like. You need to be in the middle of the emotion to really get the full benefit from this process—don't put it off until later. Honor yourself, your inner truth and how that feeling wants to be expressed and heard. What are the colors, and the shapes? Paint until you feel or sense that you are finished, or that something inside has moved or shifted. Monitor your own inner critic by not judging the outcome. This is *your* self-expression!

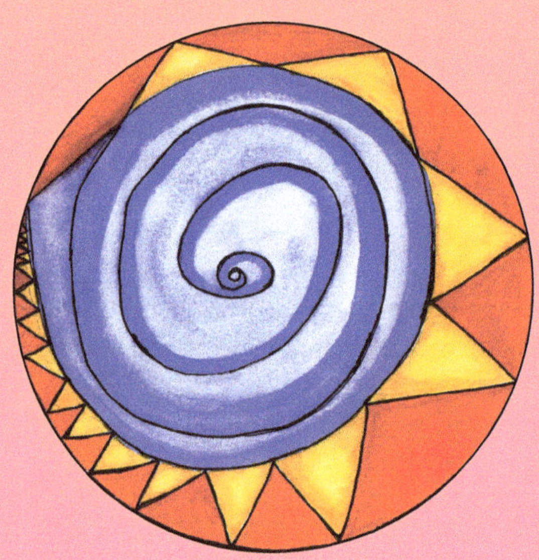

Phyllis Hill, *Unfolding*, watercolor, black felt pen

"Every time I tried to draw anything, I felt physically ill, and I desperately wanted to overcome my fear of drawing. Upon learning of my daughter's marriage breakup, I decided to use the feelings that came up to create this image. I drew for 3 weeks and the completion of this drawing brought me a welcome release."

– Phyllis Hill

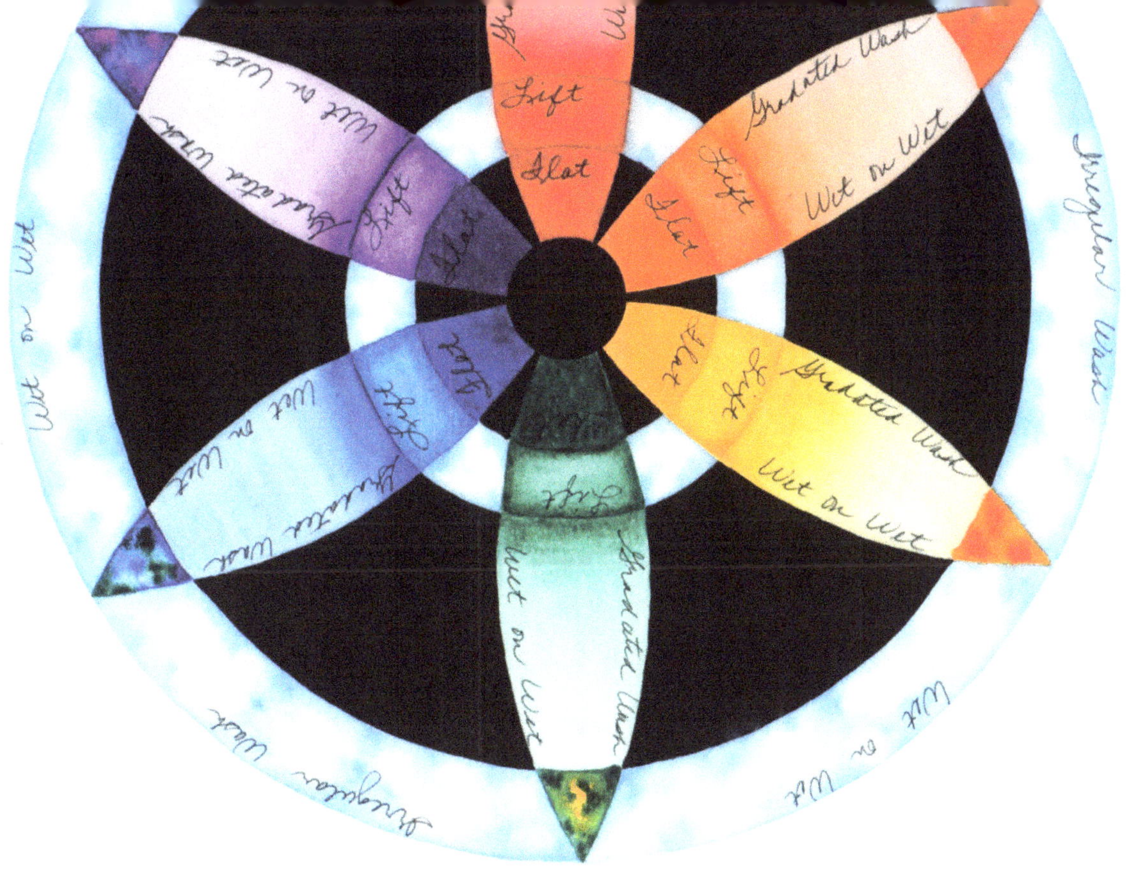

CHAPTER FOUR

Creating A Wheel Of Color

Color In Your Life

I was crazy about color at a very young age. I still remember in kindergarten painting with poster paints mixed in cut-off milk cartons. The color was rich and bright and smelled so wonderful. I could paint however I wanted, and it made me very happy. Wouldn't it have been great if painting like this would have been offered again in school?

This chapter is not only about watercolor in our mandalas, but also about color in our lives. I have found when I am painting with watercolor, my color awareness comes alive. In other words, I wake up. It seems to happen to most everyone. Color is all around us, but how often do we focus on just the color of things? Start painting in watercolor and that will change, everything will appear to become brighter and more alive. Color in our lives is such a great gift—especially when we think about what color really is—it's the sensation of light waves stimulating our eye. It's waves of light—it's energy!

As part of learning to paint mandalas, I suggest that everyone try a color wheel like the ones we used to do in art class. Color wheels provide a perfect structure in which to practice the watercolor washes from Chapter One, and they are essentially mandalas—circular, centered and symmetrical. I have painted lots of color wheels through the years, and still enjoy creating newer variations and watching them evolve.

In class the color wheels really began to change when we started meditating and chanting. It was then that I realized that our exercises were far more than color wheels. In fact, they were "wheels of color," a way to focus on and become aware of light and color in our personal lives. Looking back, I see that the color wheels were evolving from flat, one-dimensional color wheel exercises, to moving, vibrating and alive wheels of light.

I have been a student of light for a long time, joining a light group in the early 1970's. That is where I started to meditate and also the class where we were all told we were "teachers in Light." I wasn't sure what "one of those" was, but we were given many lessons about light, and, even today, not a day goes by without me using the light in some way.

We also learned about color which came in lessons from St. Germaine. "Each being would be poor indeed if he were not a receptacle of color," he said. "Remove all color and then answer the question 'What is Color?'"[1]

The color wheel mandala *Bringing in the Light* came to me in meditation and made me curious to know more about color. I decided to ask St. Germaine myself. To my surprise the following flowed as I wrote:

"You have been given the message, all things have color and radiate it. Watch for that in your life—and bring in that color for your own healing. It's a matter of noticing. And receiving. The Wheels of Color are tools for the study of color in each individual's life. And, of course, all colors come to a point in the center of all creation, and in the center of Self. When that color comes to the center of your being notice what happens. It transforms. Use that as a daily meditation and a walking meditation. See the light in all things. It is for you—and it is you. You are light many times brighter than you know. Bring light in, and reflect it out. Life is about bringing all to the center and transforming it and sending it out again from the center. What do you think you are? But a transformer of energy, raising the vibration of energies that come to you and being energized and raised yourself. Being a connector between heaven and earth, you are much needed on your world. Open up to and enjoy your function that you have chosen by being here. GOD BLESS! Circles within circles, patterns within patterns, all connected, all moving, changing spheres of light and color. You are most beautiful. If you could but see yourself you would understand the beauty of it ALL."

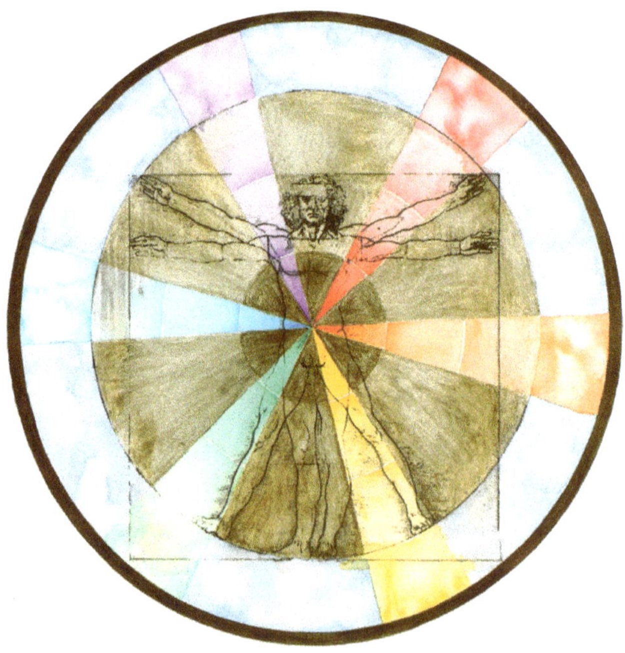

Bringing In The Light, watercolor, ink transfer, gold ink

I saw this image in meditation. The rays of rainbow colored light came to a point in the "center of man," man representing all humankind. I believe it shows the potential of color and light within us all.

CREATE YOUR OWN DESIGN

Create your own color wheel and design it any way you'd like. The more fun you have, the more likely you'll do it—and we can all use the practice. Try forgetting the compass and drawing a color wheel free hand as in *Color Wheel Drawn Free Hand*. Or paint one without drawing first. The broader the definition of color wheel, the happier it makes us all. There are no limits here and no rules.

"Show your colors," I heard one day in meditation. According to Webster's, that means to "reveal one's true self."[2] I say the same to you now.

You are light, you are energy, you are color—show your colors! Go beyond the perimeters of this exercise and have fun experiencing yourself as light and color. What color are you today? What color do you need today? Experiment with it. Enjoy it. Color, as Einstein once said, is one of the last great mysteries.

> *"Creativity is God energy*
> *flowing through us,*
> *shaped by us, like light,*
> *flowing through a crystal prism."*
> –Julia Cameron

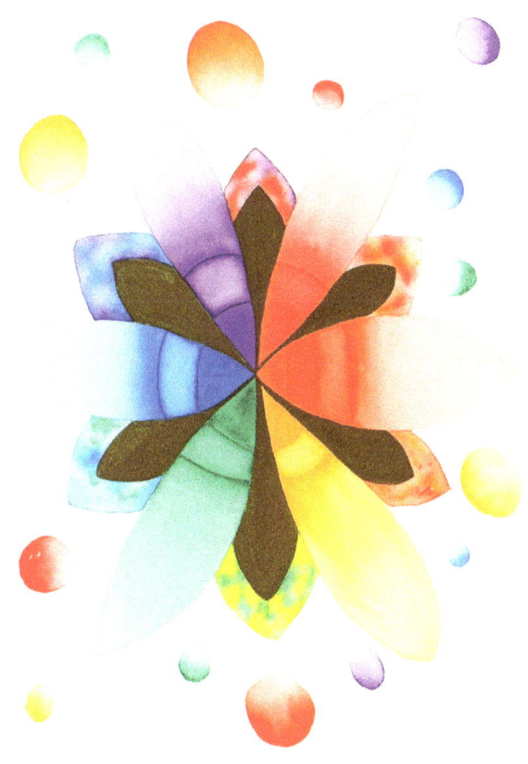

Color Wheel Drawn Free Hand, watercolor, gold ink,

This was so much fun to do and so very freeing
to work without the compass.

HOW TO CREATE A BASIC COLOR WHEEL

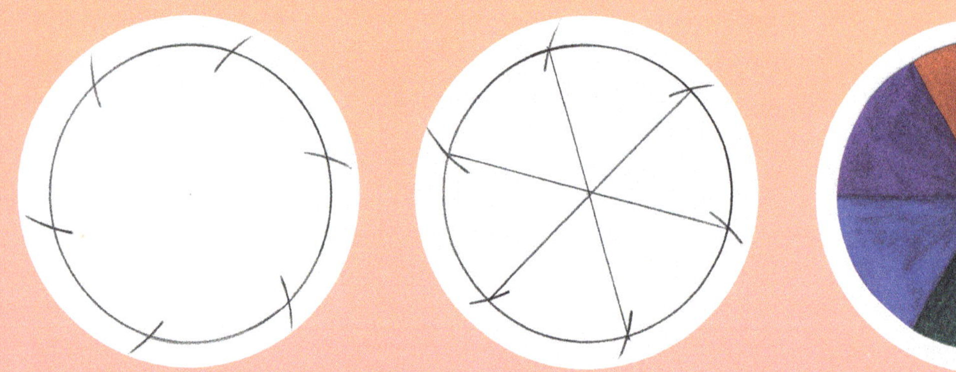

Diagram for Creating a Basic Color Wheel

LET'S START WITH THE BASICS: how to make a color wheel. It begins as a circle drawn with a compass and divided into six equal parts—which we all learned how to do in school, right? Just in case you need to refresh your memory, you may want to practice this on a piece of scratch paper before you draw it on your watercolor paper.

Get out your compass and adjust it to the size of circle you desire. Draw a circle with the compass in the middle of your paper. Do not change the compass adjustment, in other words, use the same radius. Place the point of the compass anywhere on the circumference, or edge of the circle, and where the pencil intersects the circle, draw a tick mark. See illustrations above. Now place the point of the compass exactly on the intersection of the first tick mark and the circumference of your circle. Make another tick mark where the pencil meets the circle's edge. Continue like this around the circle until you come to where you began, and you will see that you've divided the circle into 6 equal parts. Now, with a ruler, draw a line connecting the tick mark on one side of the circle to the tick mark exactly opposite it on the other side of the circle, or 3 lines connecting 6 points. You should have a circle that looks like a pie, divided into 6 equal wedges. Erase the tick marks.

This is the structure for the basic color wheel. When painting it, every other wedge or triangle is a primary color, or, red, yellow and blue. The mixture of each of those colors with each other creates secondary colors; orange is made from the mixture of equal parts of red and yellow; yellow and blue make green; blue and red make violet. On the color wheel the secondary colors go in-between the primaries. If you'd like, paint a color wheel like this just for the practice. A color wheel is painted with flat washes. Let each color dry before you paint the color right next to it, or they will bleed together. And, it's best to do light colors first and let them dry, as sometimes a darker color will bleed into a lighter color if you paint the darker color first, even if it's dry. Notice, also, that secondary colors which come directly out of the tubes are brighter than if you mix them. That's just their nature, but give mixing a try and see what fun, different colors you come up with. (When you mix a primary color with a secondary color you get what is called a tertiary color; red-violet, blue-green, etc.) Remember, these color wheels are simply for practicing your washes, not making them perfect. Get used to the feel of the brushes, the paint, the washes, mixing colors and working within the circle. Handling watercolor, by its nature, gets easier with practice. Be patient with yourself.

CREATING THE FLOWER OF LIFE COLOR WHEEL

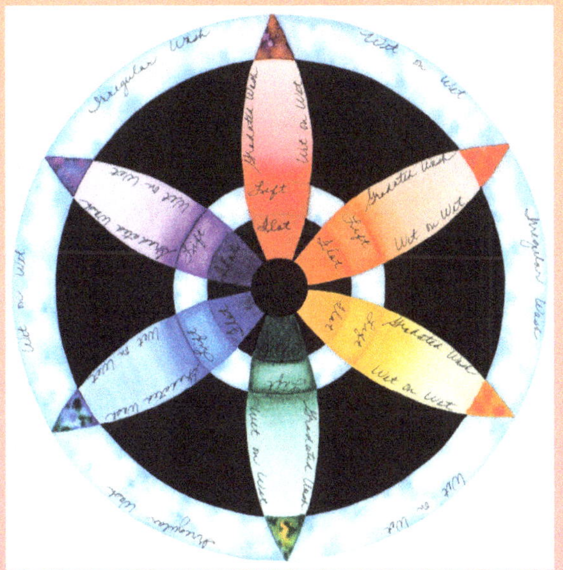

Flower of Life Color Wheel Demo

AN INTERESTING VERSION of the color wheel is the "flower of life" design. I teach this as either a design on its own, or a springboard for other creations. Give it a try, use it as a starting point for a larger design, or invent your own.

I suggest trying this first on a piece of scratch paper. With your compass draw a circle on your paper as large as you wish. Using the same radius as the circle you've just circumscribed, make six tick marks to divide the circle six times. Now, again using the compass with the exact same radius, place the point of the compass on a tick mark where it's intersected the circle. Connect the two tick marks on either side of this mark with the compass by drawing an arch between them with the pencil. Continue around the circle, placing the compass point on each tick mark and connecting the tick marks on either side of it by drawing an arc with the compass. When all the tick marks have been connected with arcs erase the tick marks. You have created a six-petal flower within a circle, which is sometimes called the "flower of life" or even the "seed of life." These designs are actually ancient and will go on infinitely if you keep drawing full circles. See illustrations below. You can change the radius of the compass and divide the petals up by circumscribing different sizes of circles over them as shown in the diagram. This gives you lots of divisions for practicing washes as in *Flower of Life Color Wheel Demo*.

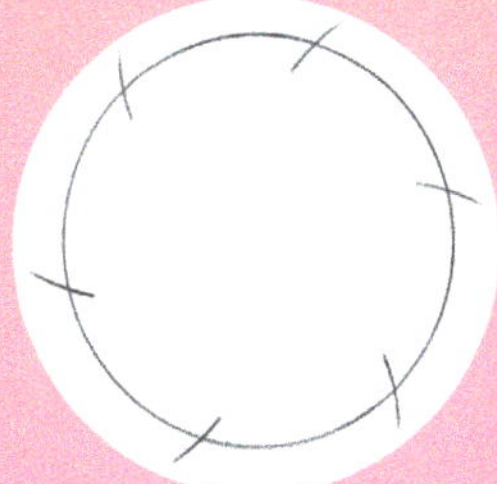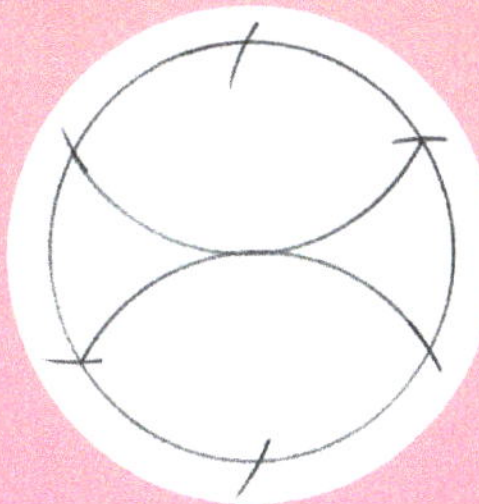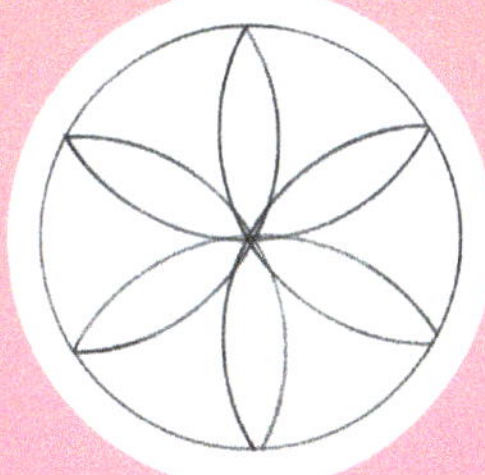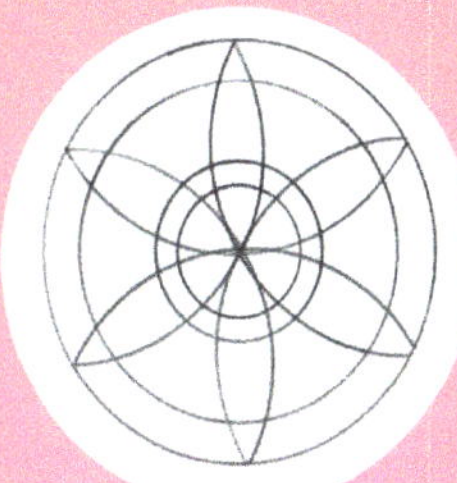

Diagram for Creating a Flower of Life Color Wheel

CREATING A WHEEL OF COLOR

HERE IS AN EXERCISE which can be used to learn about the gift of color in your life. Your intention could be for healing, or peace or to understand your personal relationship with color. Begin by writing your intention on the back of your paper. Write it as you would like, opening to and exploring all the possibilities of what you could learn about color. You can start with the basic intention which I often use: "I intend to co-create with spirit a Wheel of Color in which to practice the watercolor washes." Then I might add something like this: "And I want to learn whatever is appropriate for me to know right now."

As your intention expands beyond the basic color wheel, let go of any pre-conceived ideas you may have of what the end result of your Wheel of Color mandala may look like. Go into meditation, and then, from the back of your paper, bring your intention into your heart and chant OM. Watch and sense what happens. You will get your own version of a Wheel of Color, according to your intention. If it becomes vibrating light or energy, trust, let go and use the light to help you paint it as best you can. It may move and change right in front of you! That's what I experienced in *Healing Color Wheel*.

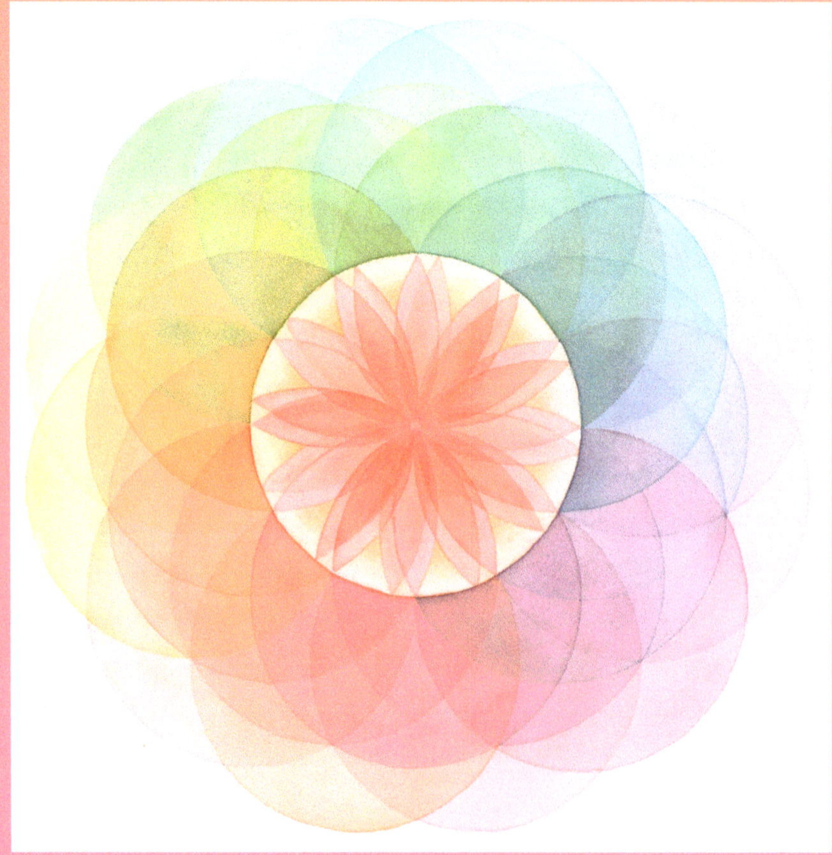

Healing Color Wheel, watercolor

I was leading a meditation during a Healing Mandala Workshop when this Wheel of Color appeared to me. It was magnificent with overlapping and swirling spheres of light. "How will I ever paint that?" I thought. It was definitely a challenge to paint but I proceeded slowly and allowed myself to learn. And what I learned was how to layer transparent washes!
I wondered, "Maybe healing happens in the same way, by going slowly and believing that you can."

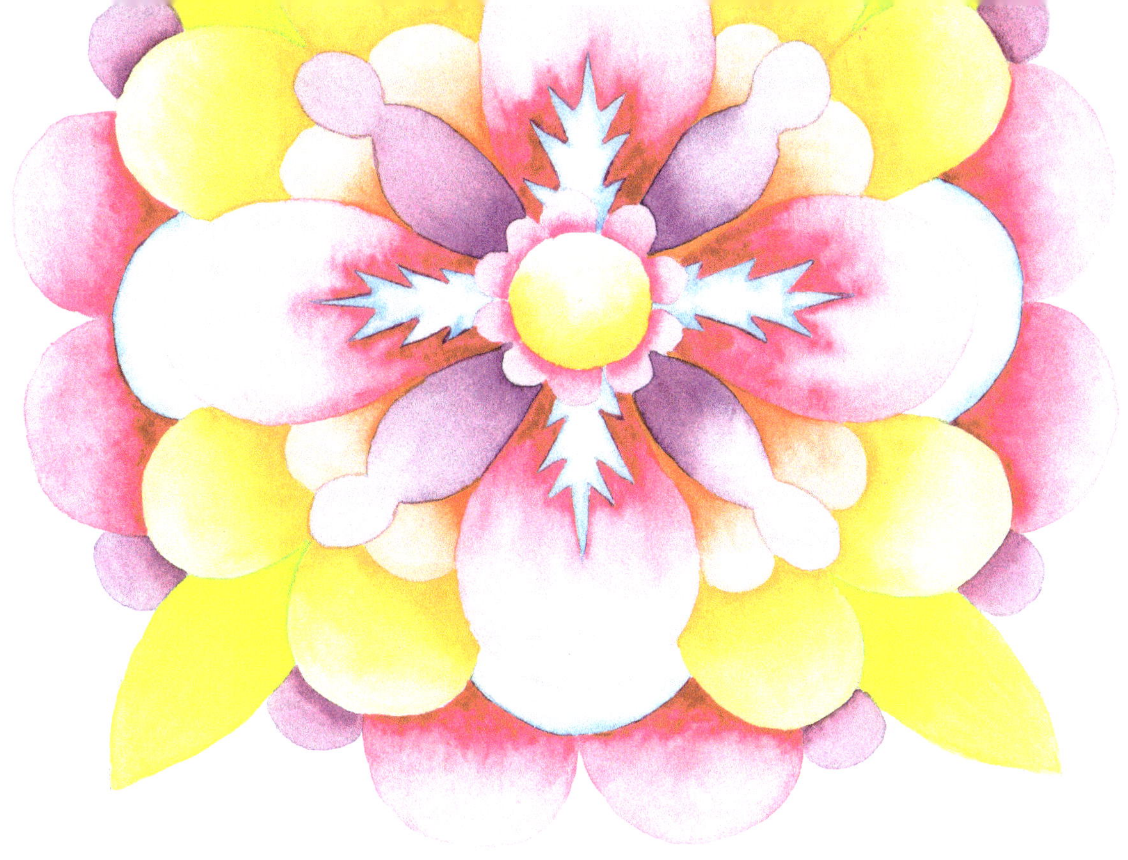

CHAPTER FIVE

THE FLOWER OF MYSELF

THE BEAUTY OF A FLOWER

"A flower.
Touch it with your love,
not just visually, but experientially.
Breathe in its aroma, it is part of you.
See its beauty, that is who you are.
Touch its softness; that is your softness.
Feel the strength of its roots.
This is your strength,
your rootedness in your world.
You would not see that flower
if it were not already a part of you."[1]

–Emmanuel

When I grew up I was surrounded by flowers. We lived in a small town in California's Central Valley. My mother grew flowers and my father grew so many vegetables in his small garden he was mentioned in *Sunset* Magazine. My mother loved her flowers and we had them everywhere.

A flower is so easy to love. It is breathtakingly beautiful, richly colorful, incredibly delicate, mysteriously fragrant, and simply one of the most splendid creations. Flowers are one of the earth's greatest gifts and greatest joys for us. Being surrounded by them is to be surrounded in love. And, to really take them in, according to this poem, is to see yourself.

That was the case for me when I experienced feeling as if I were a flower and painted my first flower mandala. See *Myself As A Flower* in How to Create A Flower Mandala on page 37. Flowers were in my blood. But I was especially curious about that flower. The barely-opening bud that I "saw," was that really me? Had I ever seen a flower like that before? What did it look like in its center? What would it look like if it fully bloomed? When I decided to try painting *Myself As A Flower*, that was the beginning of my opening to the powerful world of the mandala.

THE FLOWER WITHIN

The process of painting this flower mandala unfolded something like this: I started in the middle of a blank sheet of watercolor paper, drew what I sensed was the center of this flower inside myself, and painted it. Notice I said sensed, because I was not really seeing the inside of the flower. My sense of the center of this inner flower was that it was iris-like, and I created that as best I could. I then moved to the next layer, and did the same with each succeeding layer. I went inside myself and the flower, sensed what was there and imagined what it looked like. I then drew it, painted it, and moved on to the next concentric layer. When I finished I was surprised and curious because I had not seen the flower beforehand. This was a new view of myself, a view from the inside. And, because of that curiosity, I was not judging it. What surprised me the most were the colors I used. I generally think of myself as a bright, primary color person, so the soft, pastel colors made me wonder about the nature of my inner self. Was I softer than I realized? Years later that flower still speaks to me and surprises me.

> *"The bud,*
> *stands for all things,*
> *even for those things that don't flower,*
> *for everything flowers, from within, of*
> *self-blessing*
> *though sometimes it is necessary*
> *to reteach a thing its loveliness,*
> *to put a hand on the brow*
> *of the flower,*
> *and retell it in words and in touch,*
> *it is lovely,*
> *until it flowers again from within,*
> *of self-blessing."* [2]
>
> –Galway Kinnell

"To reteach a thing its loveliness" is the nature of the Buddhist practice *metta*, or lovingkindness. In

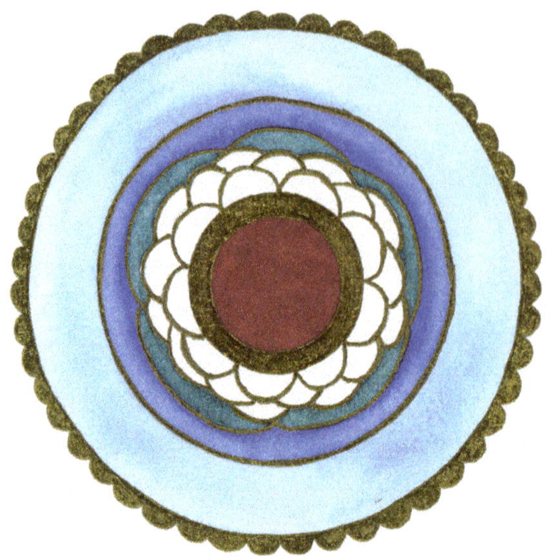

Sacred Self Flower, watercolor, gold felt pen

In the early days of painting mandalas, sometimes I would sense only a color in the center of myself, nothing more, and it was most often red. I would start from there and work outward, not within a pre-drawn circle, trusting that the mandala would unfold as a circle on its own. It always did.

her book, *Lovingkindness, The Revolutionary Art of Happiness*, Sharon Salzberg says, "Through lovingkindness everyone and everything can flower again from within. When we recover knowledge of our own loveliness and that of others, self-blessing happens naturally and beautifully." [3]

The center of many Tibetan mandalas is a stylized lotus in bloom, which is rich in symbolism. Born from the mud, this flower reaches above the mud and the water, toward the light, to unfold in pure splendor. A flower, according to the *Dictionary of All Scriptures and Myths*, "is a symbol of the virtues with which the soul is potentially endowed, and which blossom to the light as the Higher Self draws them forth...." [4] Flowers have come to represent for me a harmonious unfolding of spiritual vision as in *Sacred Self Flower*. John McCaffrey, an electrical engineer and one of my students, said of his flower *Gratitude*, "Gratitude; thanking God for everything you have and everything you don't have, leads to fulfillment."

WORKING IN AN OPEN CIRCLE

A word about the circle format. I have mentioned that when I first began mandalas I did not draw a circle and work within it. I worked from the center of the paper outward with the intention of keeping the mandala loosely circular. You can work whatever way is most comfortable for you. Many students feel, as I did at the beginning, that they just can't be confined to the circle. At a mandala workshop with Judith Cornell, she saw how I was working and commented, "You don't want the energy to leak out, keep your circle closed." I pondered on that for months afterward and began to try drawing the circle first. Finally I experienced what she meant and began to understand. Working on mandalas can be an alchemical-like process. Within the circle is you, your sacred space. As you work on yourself and process your feelings and experiences, things heat up. I see the circle as a kind of cooking pot. In it are individual ingredients, which when cooked, become something new, like a beautiful stew. Using heat and pressure, the ancient alchemists worked to change base metals into gold. But if the energy "leaks out," the transformation may be slowed, or not happen at all. In my case I was not ready to close the circle until I was ready. Do what suits you best and is most comfortable. Karen Cole's *Self As Flower* is a beautiful open circle mandala which also works as a wheel of color.

WORKING IN A CLOSED CIRCLE

Another reason I am more capable now of working within the circle is that I often see many mandalas complete, in meditation, before I begin. When I first began mandalas I did not. I worked either from pieces I would see, or from a feeling level—how I felt in my center and how I thought that might look. I really enjoyed working this way, which I did for about 3 years. I saw parts, I felt parts, and I sensed other parts. And I certainly found in mandalas an appropriate place to finally use my active imagination. But, with continued work on mandalas and deeper meditations, especially the addition of chanting, I began to see more and more full images. I have to say that when this happened I went through a period of frustration. Which way should I do mandalas? My old way, which I loved and I knew well, or this newly developing way, which I found hard because I saw what they *should* look like. That was tough to work through for me because, at first, I felt internal pressure to represent the vision perfectly and exactly as I saw it. I firmly believe people have to do what is most comfortable for them. For me, that's what I did. I stayed with the old, familiar way—at least, for a time!

ASKING FOR HELP FROM SPIRIT

Still struggling with which way I was going to do my mandalas, I attended a second Judith Cornell workshop held at Esalen Institute. It was a colored pencil drawing workshop and I found I just couldn't do the assignments she gave. So I

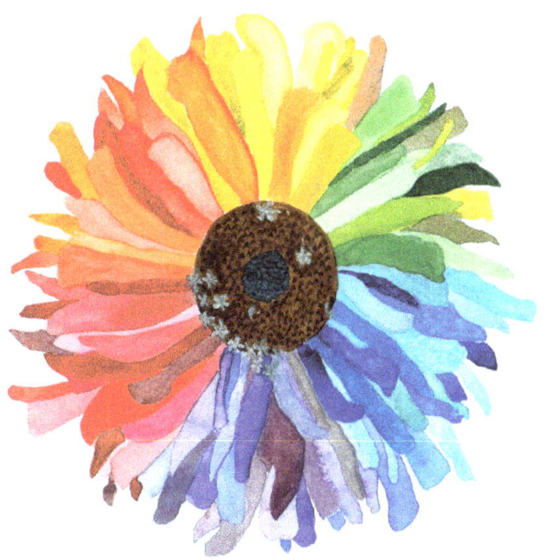

Karen Cole, *Flower of Myself*, watercolor, silver ink

Karen was an elementary school teacher who taught her students to make flower mandalas and creative color wheels. In this mandala she combines both.

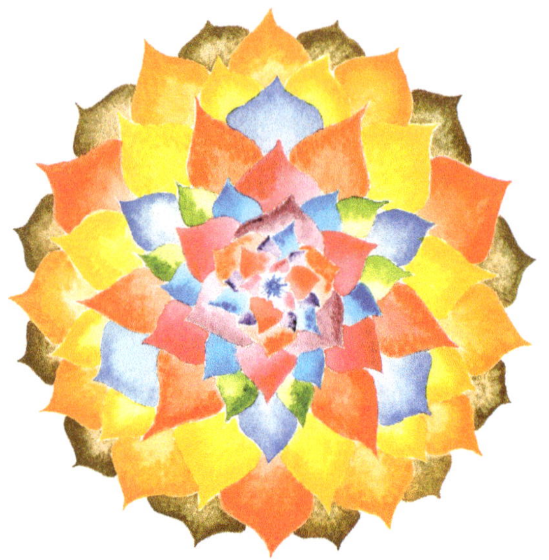

John McCaffrey, *Gratitude*, watercolor, gold ink

John did not draw his mandalas before painting them. Here he started in the middle and painted each individual petal around the center over the top of very lightly pre-drawn concentric circles. He used the wet on wet technique carefully so the colors would not bleed together.

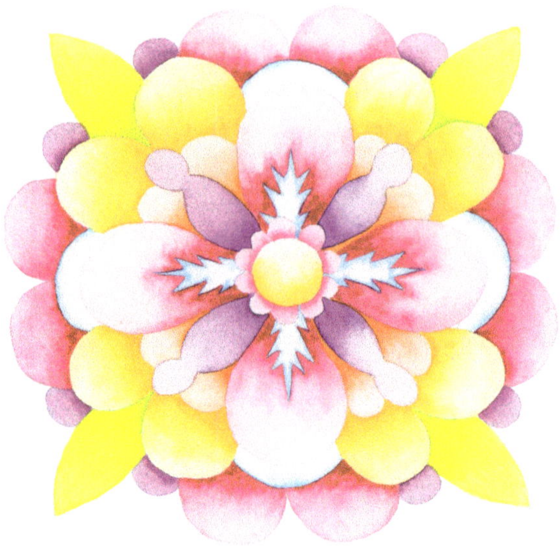

Myself: Multi-Layered, Multi-Colored, watercolor

This was a very fun mandala for me to do. My intention was to create a pink flower of myself which would represent the various colors and layers of my being. I started in the center and drew and then painted each concentric layer before I moved on to the next. It's always fascinating to see what will be created.

went to my room to paint, not draw, mandalas, but found I could do neither. I felt completely frustrated and stumped. What now? Because I was there for five days, that being the first day, and not wanting to waste my money, I decided to ask for help—from Spirit. I was given a vision of the etheric light of a flower that was so involved, complicated and shimmering that I didn't know where to begin. So, step by step, I surrendered, asked for help, and was guided as to how to proceed, with the pencils, and I did it! This taught me an invaluable lesson. It's not about finding or following one way of doing things. It's about spirit giving me the confidence to be the best and do the best that I can, to be my Highest Self and let go to it. And to let go of the fear. This is what mandalas are for me.

Within my circle, my sacred space, I find the spirit of my true self and the energy to follow it. And that doesn't mean my mandalas always remain the same, done the same way or in the same style. They change and have continued to change. What's important is that I follow the energy, which is always asking me to let go to it and trust. So sometimes I paint very precisely, other times freely and spontaneously, whatever my inner self needs at the time. Sometimes I see full visions beforehand, and sometimes I don't. For that reason, I paint in different ways and my mandalas don't all have a certain "look." They may even appear to have been done by different people. Well, as it is said, things are not always as they appear. I'm not trying for a style—I'm trying to be true to myself, the energy and spirit.

How did the drawing class at Esalen turn out? I did continue to enjoy learning and drawing with the colored pencils which I used years later in mandalas, layered over the watercolor. However, I couldn't pass the opportunity to paint at least one flower that spoke to me. *There Are Worlds Within Worlds* is that painting which is at the end of the chapter. That little viola said it wanted to be BIG.

HOW TO CREATE A FLOWER MANDALA

A FLOWER is such a beautiful symbol of ourselves. "To flower is to bloom and to reach the best."[5] This mandala exercise is to see yourself as a fully blooming flower which you are observing from above. Most flowers are mandala-like when you look at them from this perspective. This flower of yourself could be real, imagined or both, as my first one was. See if you can let go and allow it to come to you in meditation. It is not uncommon to have an idea of what you think you'd like to paint and in meditation receive something entirely different. So, begin by writing your intention on the back of your piece of watercolor paper. "I intend to co-create with spirit the flower of myself" or, "I intend to have fun painting myself as a fully blooming flower." Go into meditation, bring your intention into your heart and follow with the OM chant. Watch what happens, or what you feel or sense. Whatever you receive, or don't receive, is exactly right for you. Trust that and begin your painting.

When you are finished with your work, hang it up in a safe place so it may continue to teach you. This is your inner work and it must be protected from those who may not understand what you are doing. I remember once my Dad looked at an iris I had painted, and thought he was so funny saying "It looks like a moose!" I like what Georgia O'Keefe says about other's comments: "Well—I made you take time to look at what I saw and when you took time to really notice my flower you hung all your associations with flowers on my flower and you write about my flower as if I think and see what you think and see of the flower—and I don't." [6]

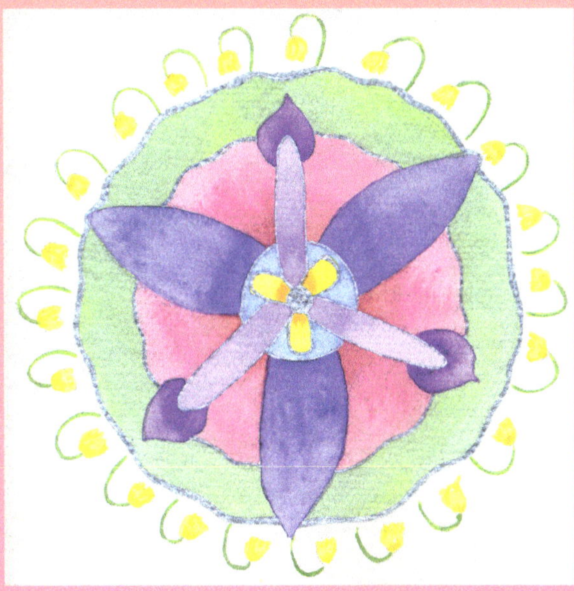

Flower of Myself, watercolor, silver pen

"Each flower is a symbol of the Infinite trying to express Itself."
—Paramahansa Yogananda

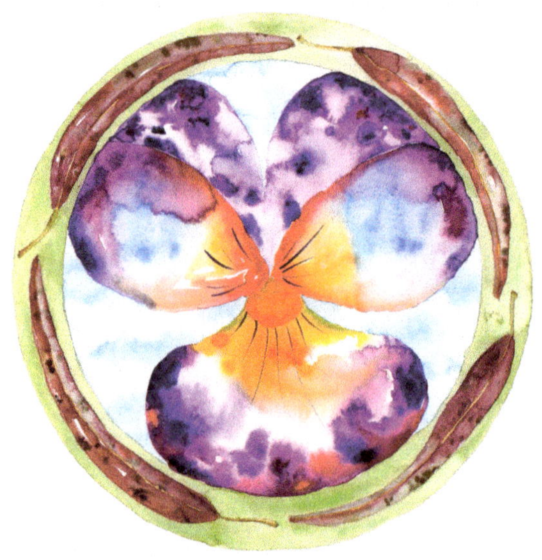

There Are Worlds Within Worlds, watercolor

This is the little flower which wanted to be big.
It became clear as I painted, that there was more to this
little flower and its world than what I could see with
my eyes. What that told me was that there was more
to me, as well, than what I appeared to be.

Flowers changed the face of the planet. Without them the world we know—even man himself—would never have existed….—Loren Eiseley

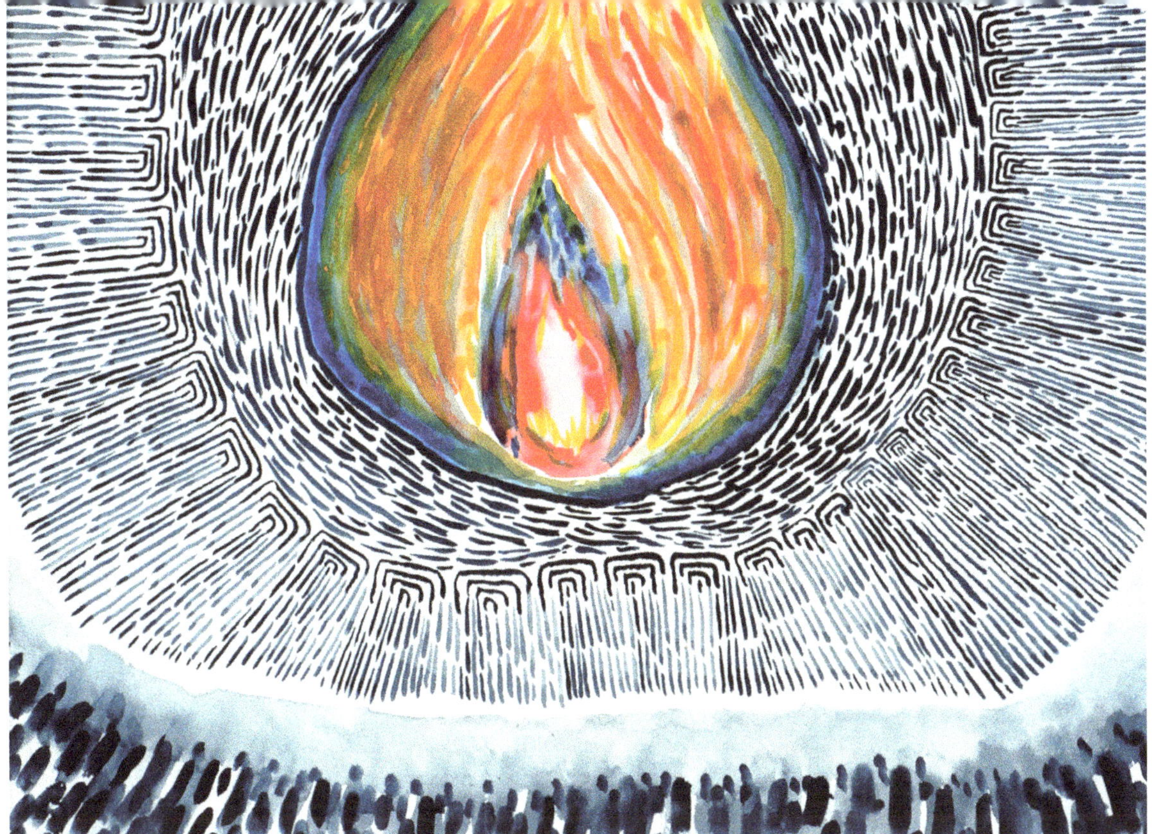

CHAPTER SIX

The Seeds Of Ourselves

The Faith In A Seed

"Though I do not believe that a plant will spring up where no seed has been, I have great faith in a seed. Convince me that you have a seed there, and I am prepared to expect wonders."[1]

–Henry David Thoreau

Seeds were like gold in California's agricultural Central Valley. As many did in those days, my father would carefully save seeds from his vegetable crops for the next season's planting. I had a small patch of ground when I was a child, and planted a few of my dad's vegetable seeds and some of my mom's flower seeds. I participated in the cycle of the seeds, learning to nurture the process from planting to harvesting which would always come full circle to the collecting of seeds for the next year. There was a security and comfort in those cycles and a feeling of abundance because the seeds were so plentiful.

Seeds are definitely one of life's mysteries. A seed holds in potential it's true nature. If nurtured properly it will grow and assume the form that is characteristic of its nature. A seed is a storehouse of innate possibility, like the acorn which holds within it the knowledge, the blueprint, and the energy to fulfill its destiny as an oak tree. And the oak tree has the potential to produce many more acorns which could root, become oak trees, and so on, infinitely.

Our Potential

This chapter is about our potential, which, like seeds, is also a wealth of possibilities. I have always envisioned that possibility, in our mandala work, as a rich seed. The seed mandala seems to call up such playfulness, imagination and creativity in most everyone. Over the years it has proven to be one the easiest mandalas for everyone to do. To coach our imagination, we ask ourselves these

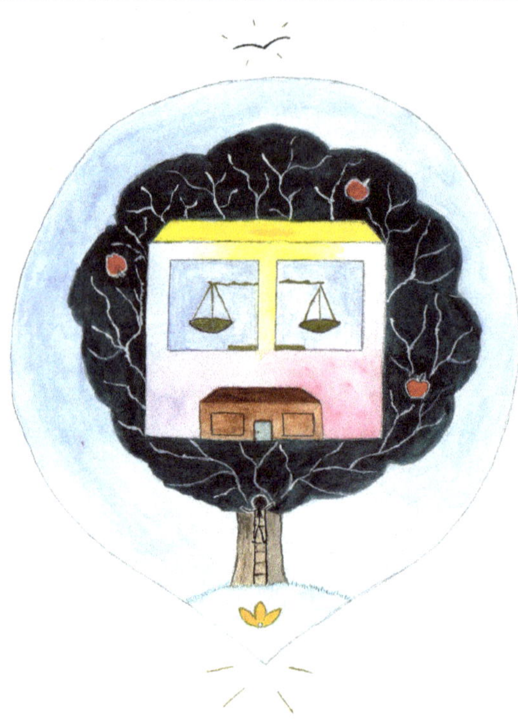

Lane Cara Shaw, *The Seed Of Possibility; Who am I? Am I being watered? Where am I?* Watercolor, gold paint

"The divine seed is each one of us. We live our lives as if in a dream—an illusion. The Reality is within us. We climb the ladder to the Tree of Knowledge. Nothing is handed-to-us-on-a-plate. We must earn our progress. We go to school in our early days, not realizing that the whole of life is a learning process. The scales seen through the windows symbolize the positive and negative energies we must learn to balance. The apples represent the blessings and help we receive on our journey. Finally, like a bird, we regain our freedom."
—Lane Cara Shaw

questions: What are the possibilities of the original seed within me and where is the seed now? What is the stage of growth that the seed of myself is in now? Is it a new sprout, a bud, a flower? Or is the flower spent and making way for the coming fruit or vegetable? Or is the seed in its winter stage, gathering strength and energy for its next cycle of growth? Have I cared and nurtured it properly? What is the potential of myself and the fulfillment of my seed destiny? These are some of the questions Lane Cara Shaw asked in her mandala *The Seed of Possibility*.

According to Zen Master Thich Nhat Hanh: "There are many kinds of seeds within us, both good and bad. Some were planted during our life-time, and some were transmitted by our parents, ancestors and our society....[They] have given us seeds of joy, peace, and happiness, as well as seeds of sorrow, anger, and so on....Each of us needs a reserve of seeds that are beautiful, healthy, strong....Every time a seed has an occasion to manifest itself, it produces new seeds of the same kind....When I smile, the seeds of smiling and joy have come up. As long as they manifest, new seeds of smiling and joy are planted. But if I don't practice smiling for a number of years, that seed will weaken, and I may not be able to smile anymore."[2]

FAITH OF THE MUSTARD SEED

With love we nourish ourselves and watch our potential grow and blossom. "I would picture myself in a wide-open field planting seeds...we plant

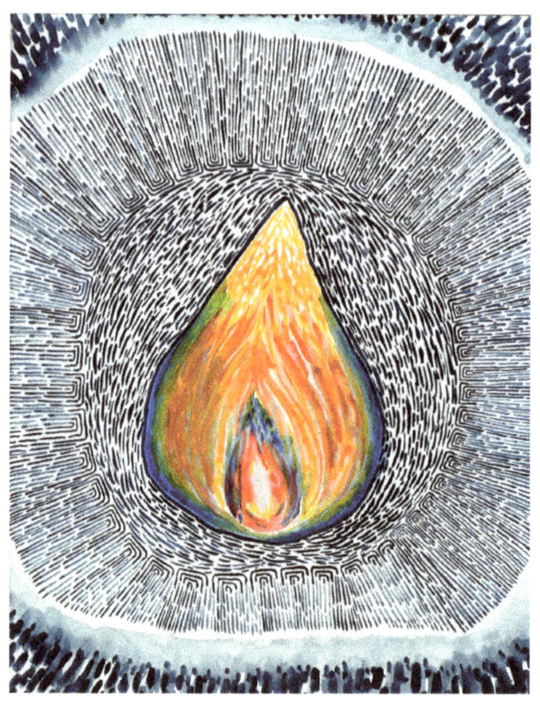

John McCaffrey, *Flame of Knowledge*, watercolor

John wrote this about his paintings:
"As we continue on the spiritual path we all come to a point of inner exploration. And when we dive into the center of our being we have experiences of the Self. These paintings are symbols of such experiences. Either a vision or a profound feeling in meditation has inspired them."

seeds of love, knowing that nature will take its course and in time those seeds will bear fruit," says Buddhist teacher Sharon Salzberg. "Some seeds will come to fruition quickly, some slowly, but our work is simply to plant seeds."[3]

When we form this intention, channeling the energies of our mind, we can trust the laws of nature to support our blossoming.

For me it's like having the faith of the mustard seed, from the parable in the Bible. In it Jesus tells his disciples that the kingdom of God is like a tiny grain of mustard seed, which is smaller than most other seeds, but once it is sown in the earth it grows bigger than most other plants. The faith of the mustard seed, which is really a seed of love, is symbolic of the faith in our expanding and awak-

SEED EXCHANGE PROJECT

During one series of classes, I had a dream in which a friend and I were exchanging seeds and bulbs from our gardens. That gave me the idea to have students paint small seeds or bulbs, and exchange them with each other, like we used to do with valentine cards on Valentine's Day. The idea was to give one of our painted "seeds" to each class member, and receive one back from everyone. Then we would "plant" these seeds—these gifts from others—by incorporating them into our next mandala.

If there is a large enough group to do so, this can be a fun project. Make a seed which represents yourself, and paint it on your watercolor paper. Keep it simple. Then cut it out so that it's about the size of a quarter. The seeds can all be different, or all the same. Exchange one with each person in the group. Now incorporate these seeds into your next mandala. It's an interesting exercise which most everyone enjoys doing. The idea here is to create some fun, play and interchange between each other. I incorporated the seeds I was given into the inner child mandala, the class assignment in the next chapter. See *The Crayola Kid*.

ening awareness of our self. See John McCaffrey's powerful *Flame of Knowledge.*

OUR MAGNIFICENCE

When speaking about mandalas, His Holiness The Dalai Lama said, "Mandala, in general, means that which extracts the essence....The main meaning is for oneself to enter into the mandala and extract an essence in the sense of receiving blessing. It is a place of gaining magnificence."[4] Within our own seed is our potential, our essence and our magnificence. With faith we enter our mandala, acknowledge our seed and, with awakened awareness, we receive blessing.

SEED MANDALAS

One of my favorite seed mandalas, *Seed of Possibility*, began with sensing the seed of myself within my own center. I placed my image of it in the center of the paper and working outward from the center, drew and then painted each layer before moving on to the next. As I finished, the poem seemed to write itself.

Yes, *I Am Chicken* <u>is</u> a seed mandala, and what a process it was. I said seed mandalas could get very imaginative. I started out innocently enough by going into meditation with my intention being "My Seed." A seed appeared, but, before I knew it, the seed became an eye, and then it became the eye of a chicken. My seed is a chicken's eye? It seemed so odd and funny that I went ahead and painted it and had a good laugh. It took a couple of days though before I realized that the eye was really "I." I had been feeling some fear, this chicken was afraid and "I" was the chicken! This coincided with asking my mother if we could meet to talk about our past. I wasn't aware that I was afraid, but my mandala showed me that I was. I had lived with a good deal of fear of my

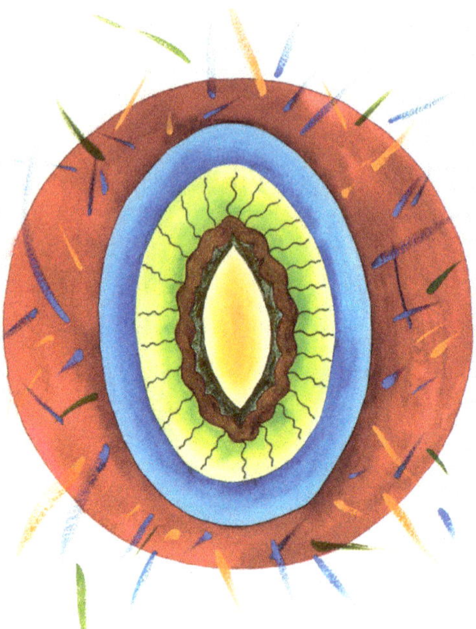

Seed Of Possibility, watercolor, gold ink, gold felt pen

After I completed this mandala, I wrote on the back:
"My inner seed glows and is surrounded by gold. It is
buried in the earth of my soul and roots take hold.
It is watered by my inner well. The cosmos
welcomes me and is my home."

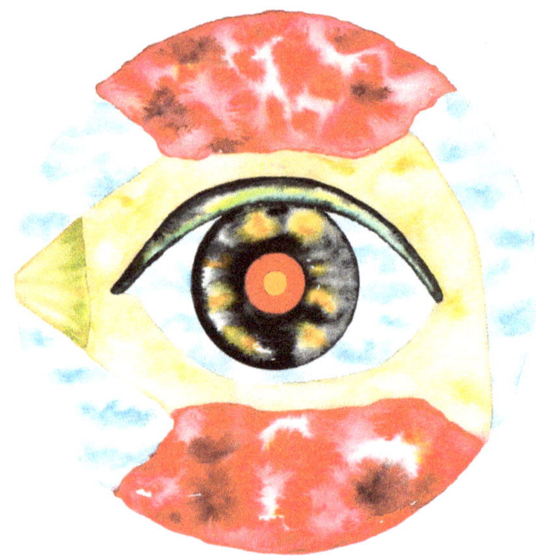

I Am Chicken, watercolor

Sometimes the inner self can be playful and fun when it
delivers its message. Here the seed was literally me, or "I."
This mandala always makes me smile!

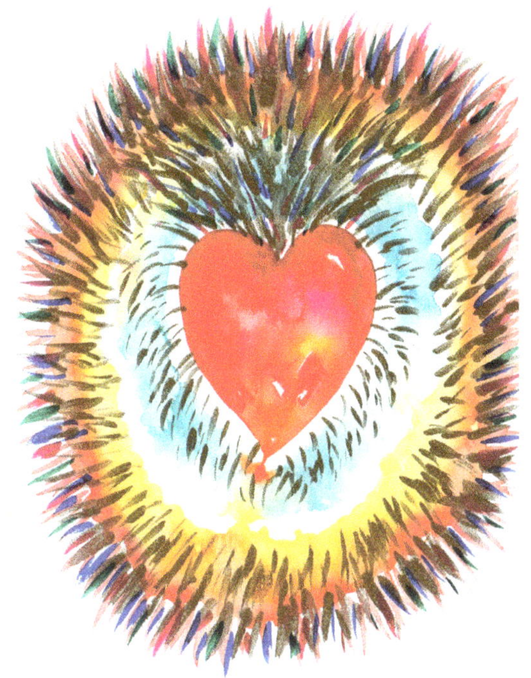

The Sacred Heart, watercolor, gold ink

This seed mandala started out as a disappointment when
I saw the heart in response to my intention. I wanted and
expected some other image to show me my seed potential.
I thought, "Another heart? Haven't I already painted
enough of them?" I think I was being shown the
sacred potential of my own heart.

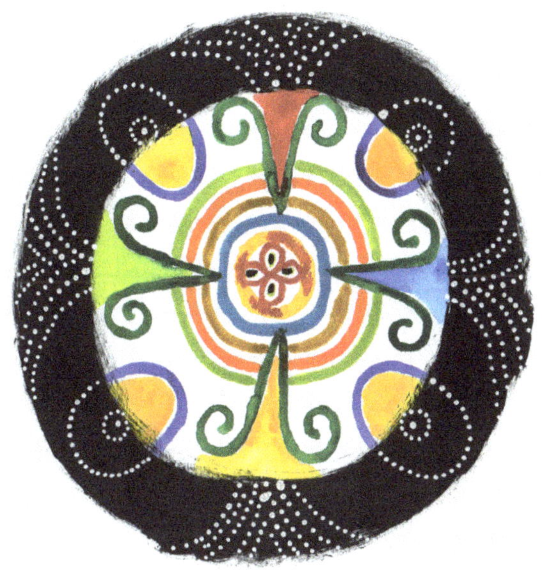

Don Faia, *Seed of Possibilities*, gouache

Don enjoyed painting in class with opaque
watercolor, or gouache. He also took every opportunity
to paint in a loose "primitive" or "native" way which he
experienced as freeing him to connect with ancient
wisdom. This mandala is very powerful with raw energy.

mother throughout my life. On the day we met, I
began to face it. I thought a lot about my family's
seeds—especially the ones sown in me.

SACRED SEED

In the mandala *The Sacred Heart* my intention
was to paint "The Potential of My Inner Seed," at
least that's what I wrote on the back of my paper.
But in meditation I saw a heart, and as I began
painting, was quickly overcome by powerful feelings of its sacredness. It was surrounded by energies of Mary as the Virgin of the Guadalupe. I felt
choked up, my own heart stuck in my throat and
I felt profoundly touched with deep love and long-
ing. I finished by dabbing on gold ink—almost as
a ceremonious offering. I love this painting now,
especially its spiritual mystery.

Both of these mandalas, my *Sacred Heart* and
my husband's *Seed of Possibilities*, represent each
of us diving into our sacred center, where the seed
potential is found, and in different ways, making a
spiritual connection. The seed mandala is a very
blessed journey and will lead you toward discovering your full potential.

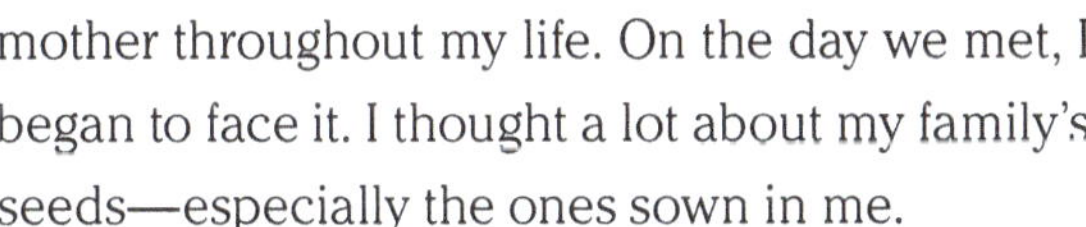

CREATING A SEED MANDALA

BEGIN BY WRITING your intention on the back of your paper. Perhaps you could state it as "I intend to co-create with spirit my seed of possibility" or "Seeing the seeds of my self today." Go into meditation, relax, ground yourself, letting the light flow and expand within you. Bring your intention into your heart and charge your intention by chanting the OM chant.

What do you find there? What do you see, feel or know about your seed? When you begin your work, see if you can stay within a circle, or loosely in a circle format. Or try working on a square piece of paper if you would like to keep your mandala symmetrical. Sometimes mandalas will grow into the size and shape of the paper you use as in the seed mandalas of Lane Cara Shaw, Karen Cole, John McCaffrey and my *The Sacred Heart*. All were painted on 11"x15" paper and grew to fill the space.

When you have completed the mandala, date your work on the back, and make any notes about your process to remember at a later time. Does it have a title? Hang it up and be with it.

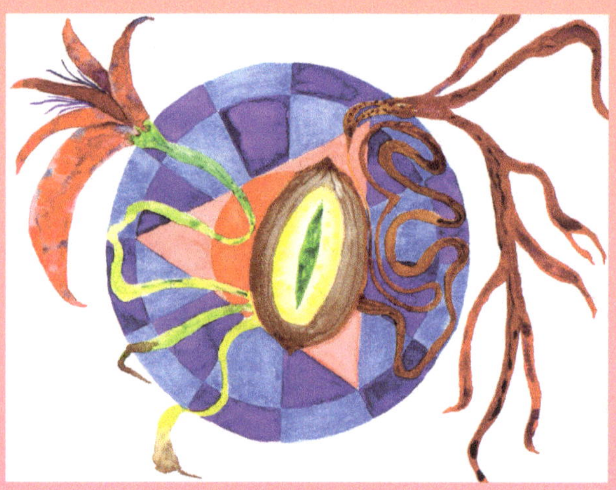

Karen Cole, *My Seed—A Possibility*, watercolor

Some mandalas can grow beyond their boundaries and become asymmetrical in their symmetry.

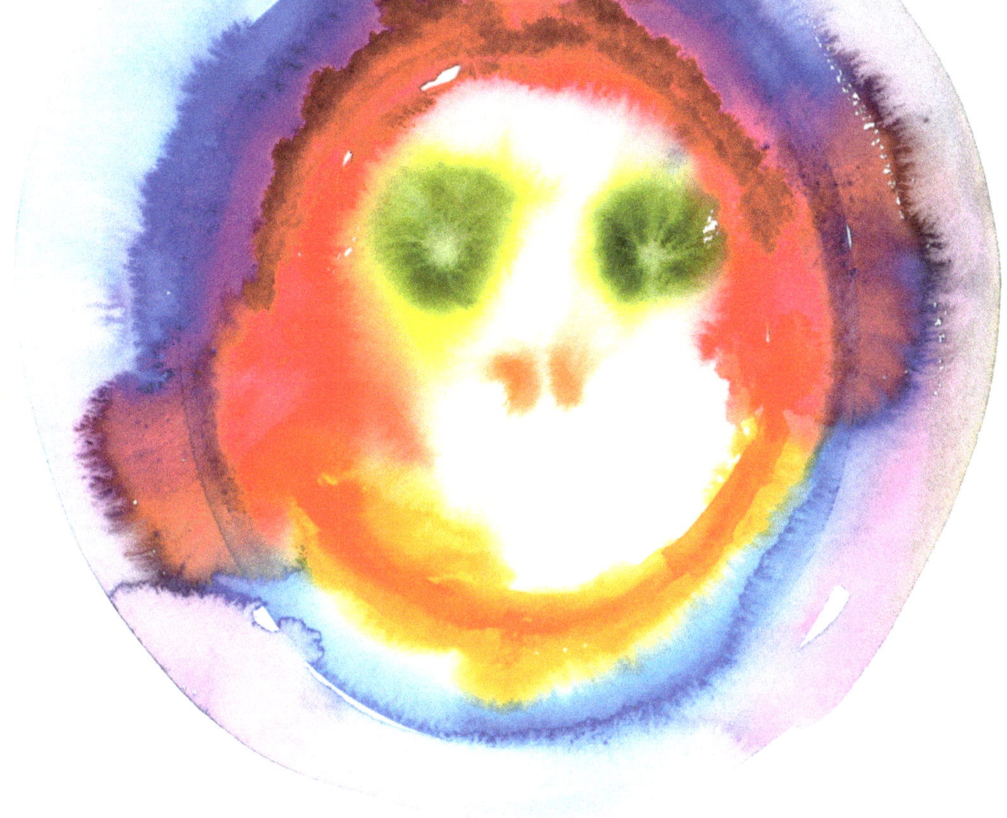

CHAPTER SEVEN

CHILD'S PLAY

LET THE CHILD OUT TO PLAY

Play is the natural state of the child. Within ourselves we all have an inner child. It is where our spontaneity, creativity and playfulness reside. We may think that when we grew up and became an adult we gave up child-like things, and the child was somehow erased from our being. Or we may have made a valiant attempt to accelerate the growing-up process, like I did, trying to become the perfect, little adult at a ridiculously young age. I thought that ridding myself of my childish ways was what was expected of me. One spiritual teacher says, "Actually, the part of you that was the infant still exists, and is a vital part of your potential as a complete human. From a new age standpoint, as well as for general human health, this is very potent....Hidden in each of you is a full blueprint of who you are....The inner child is the gateway to its revelation."[1]

Here's that seed of potential again and it is found in the inner child. Now it's time to let that child out to play. This chapter's mandala is about letting go, having fun and experiencing what that feels like. Play heals!

Many of us may feel that if we were to let our child out, we might feel as if we were regressing and negating our mature, adult self. But if we look at the art work of many revered artists from our history, such as Picasso, Chagall, Klee or Miro, we see that they knew the value and importance of their child-like innocence and strove for it in their creative work. Picasso once said that it took him his whole life to become young again.

ESSENCE OF THE INNER CHILD

Accessing the inner child is to connect with the magic, freedom, joy, and the uncomplicated and worry-free spirit of being young. It is being

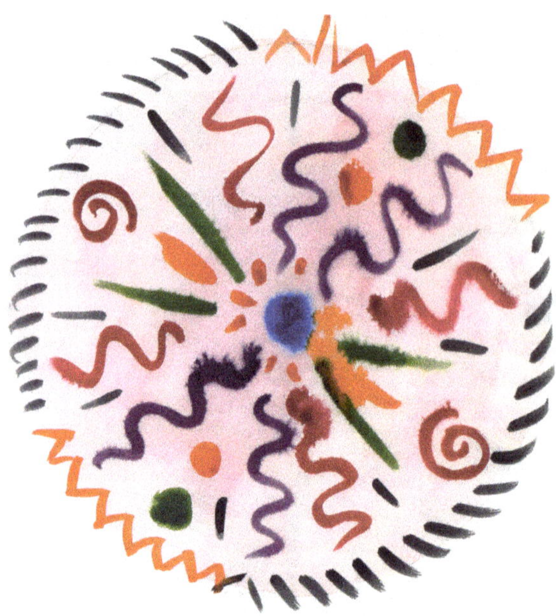

Jennifer Field, *Magic Of The Inner Child III*, watercolor

This fun and alive mandala was painted very simply
and quickly with Jennifer's non-dominant hand.

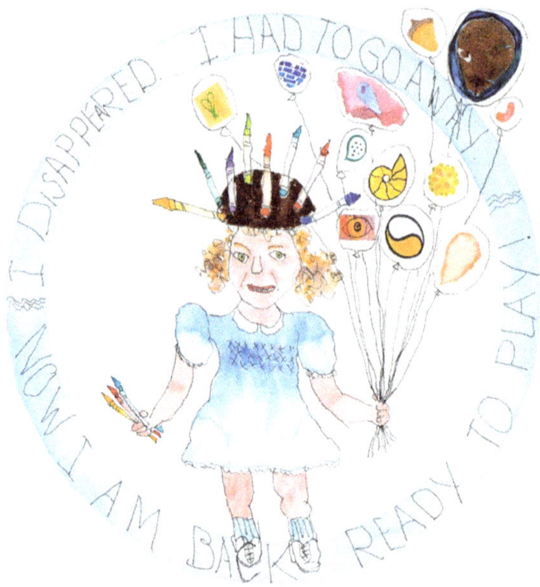

The Crayola Kid, watercolor, foil, collage pieces

Drawn with my non-dominant hand and painted with
the other, this was FUN! It felt good to let the old hurtful
memory go by painting my child empowered with her
crayons. She says, "I disappeared, I had to go away,
now I am back, ready to play."

full of curiosity and laughter, and doing what
you really want, rather than what you think you
should do. It is not caring what others think. It is
being self-accepting and self-trusting. It is being
happy about who you are with no self-doubt. It is
about just being.

Depak Chopra says, "A baby comes into this
world from the very source of life, and it detaches
from that source gradually....Innocence remains
intact in a state of purity and wholeness that you
simply forget."[2]

The essence of the child remains within, it is
simply forgotten. And what is the essence of the
child but the remembrance it carries from where
it came from, the "very source of life." The essence
of the inner child is truly its divinity. Feelings of
the inner child in an adult can "foster peace, and
a lack of fear....They suspend time and aging and
bring you face to face with your higher self...if you
let them."[3]

ACCESSING THE INNER CHILD

In my mandala work I have found one of the
quickest, easiest and most fun ways to get in
touch with my inner child is by drawing or painting with my non-dominant hand. Believe me, it
works and it is fun. I can hear the moans now, "I
can't do that!" Consider giving it a try as Jennifer
Field did in *Magic of the Inner Child III*. Let yourself be free. Let go of control for a few minutes.
When I teach this class the giggling is contagious
and everyone starts to play. Lucia Capacchione
has written extensively about the inner child in
Recovery of Your Inner Child and about using your
non-dominant hand in *The Power of Your Other
Hand*. I recommend them both.

Our inner child truly has a wealth of energy,
wisdom and creativity and it's all alive inside each
one of us.

POWERFUL FEELINGS EMERGE

When called upon, my inner child seems to have no hesitations when it comes to drawing and painting mandalas. Powerful feelings emerge, the strength and power of which surprise me. I feel free and it's very self-entertaining. Usually the child doesn't care what the work looks like, nor what the outcome is. I say "usually" because sometimes the adult judge will try to get in there and be critical. At those times this critical part of myself must be told that I am busy with work that is very important to me, that criticism is not helpful, and to leave me for now. Sometimes uncomfortable feelings may emerge, and I let myself go with them. I feel that whatever comes up is important, should not be held back, and needs to be honored, accepted and gently walked through.

OLD ART WOUNDS

Just before I painted the inner child mandala *The Crayola Kid*, I had had a dream about "my little girl" disappearing. Since I don't have a little girl, I knew it was my inner child. In the dream a neighbor had offered to help me find her, telling me the way to do so was to meditate. For me the message was clear, I needed to "find" her, so I began a mandala. My intention, which I took into meditation, was: "Inner child mandala; drawing with left hand and incorporating seeds from the class." See the Seed Exchange Project from the previous chapter. What surfaced in meditation was myself as a 4-year-old, wearing the dress that I had innocently soiled when I'd put crayons in my lap while coloring. My mother had punished me by taking away my crayons, confusing me as to why my "important work" had been taken away. It deeply affected me and I refer to this incident now as my "original art wound." Sadly, I am discovering, too many of us have traumas around our early art work. These come from things that are said or done to us which drive our creative self deep inside, to hide from embarrassment or humiliation. Gently reconnecting with our creative self in mandala work can be an empowering way to heal these old traumas.

WORKING WITH FACILITATORS

I have found inner child work to be very important for my health, and that is why at times I have worked with both a bodywork facilitator and a psychotherapist. I release emotions and energy that have been stuffed or blocked in my body, allowing me to be more and more alive. I mention this because I feel that with such rich and potent work, a facilitator of some kind is a great gift to oneself, and I recommend it. I often would bring a mandala to a session, not so much to be discussed, but because it helped me with my own clarity, and I knew it was a safe place, free of judgement. Sometimes in the session, the mandala image would suddenly surface somewhere in my body, and that would always deepen the work and bring further insight to both the image and my inner self.

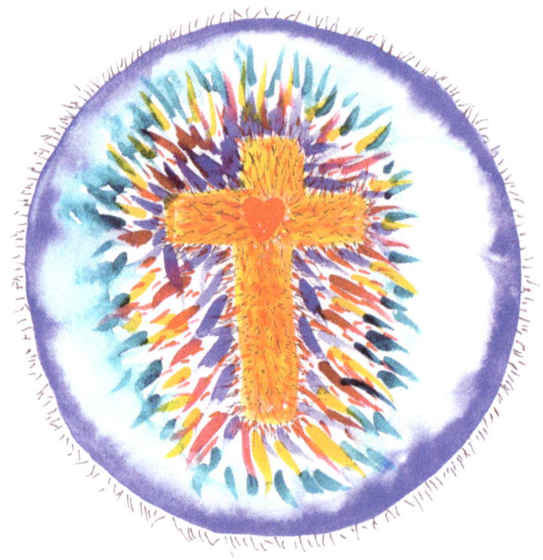

The Cross That Keeps Coming Up, watercolor, gold pen

When I saw the cross again and again, I realized how comforting Sunday School was as a child—and my faith. I also realized how hard that had been for me to admit for fear of ridicule. This was painted with my non-dominant hand.

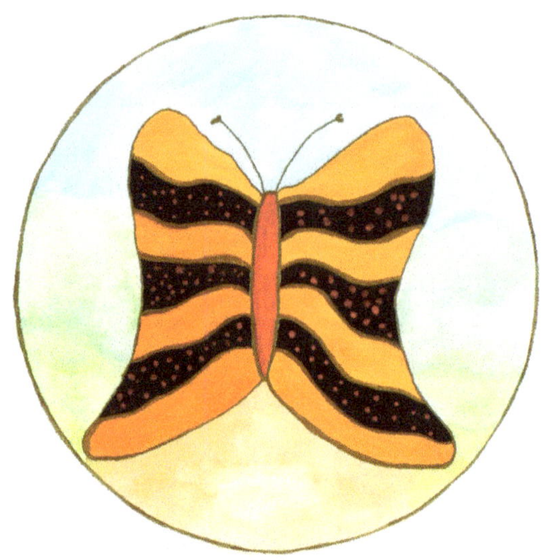

Meris Walton, *Connecting with the Inner Child* watercolor, gold pen

Meris, a chiropractor and mother of three boys, drew this with her non-dominant hand and painted with her dominant hand.

In *The Crayola Kid* my creative child resurfaced boldly. I proceeded to draw her with my left hand, quite easily and quickly, and painted her with my right. She was back, in all her glory, with her crayons! I felt giddy and happy. I also had a new-found energy and confidence around drawing, having always felt I could never draw quite "right." Drawing like this was just too much fun to matter if it was correct or perfect. The "balloons" she's carrying are the "seeds" made by members of the seed mandala class mentioned on page 41 in the previous chapter.

SECURITY OF A REMEMBERED PLACE

When you let the child out "there takes place a cellular remembrance of the place you came from...and the security of that place."[4] I learned about that when I was leading a meditation during an inner child mandala class. Although I had not planned on painting with everyone that day, I felt emotionally compelled to paint an image of a cross which came to my awareness, seen in *The Cross That Keeps Coming Up*. Many childhood memories flooded my consciousness—warmth, love, security and trust. I didn't want to paint the cross and I kept trying to push it away. My inner child wouldn't let me. The image persisted, and when I reluctantly accepted it, I was overwhelmed with feelings of old, deep love and security. It was quite powerful and revealing, especially when almost unconsciously I heard myself say, "I want to heal." Acceptance was needed for healing.

Inner child mandalas can be very, very powerful, and really lots of fun. It's such a relief not to have to be an adult all of the time! These mandalas can give us much-needed balance and a lot of pleasure. Meris Walton's butterfly is so delightful in her mandala *Connecting With The Inner Child*.

How To Get Started
On An Inner Child Mandala

BEGIN BY WRITING YOUR INTENTION on the back of your paper. For example, "I intend to co-create with spirit an inner child mandala," or "I intend to have fun letting my child play." Or, write it in any way that sounds fun and inviting to your child within. Go into meditation, bring your intention into your heart, chant the OM chant and then notice any feelings or movement within as the child makes its way to the forefront of your awareness. Draw a circle with your compass, and try to work within the circle, or at least in a circular format. You can draw your mandala first with your non-dominant hand, which is how I first began. You can also really let loose and paint directly, just as a child would do. I originally would draw with my left hand (my non-dominant hand) and then paint with my right hand. But now I've "progressed" in my inner child mandalas, and paint with my left-hand without drawing first.

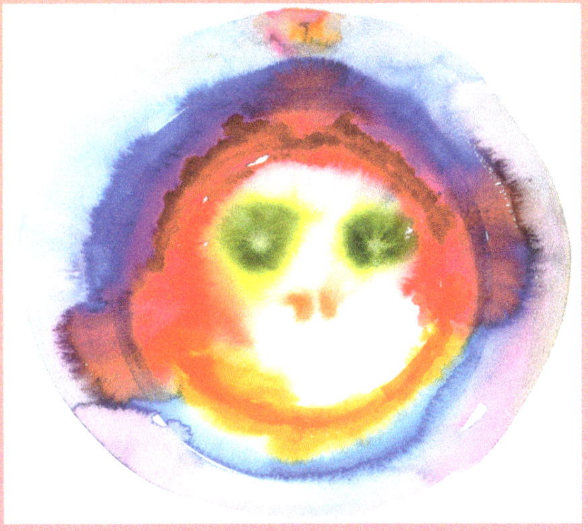

Frappé, watercolor

When I painted this quick mandala and saw the playful
face, I laughed and said, "Where did you come from?"
More than one face has appeared in my mandalas
and I have always been happy to welcome the inner
being and make its acquaintance.

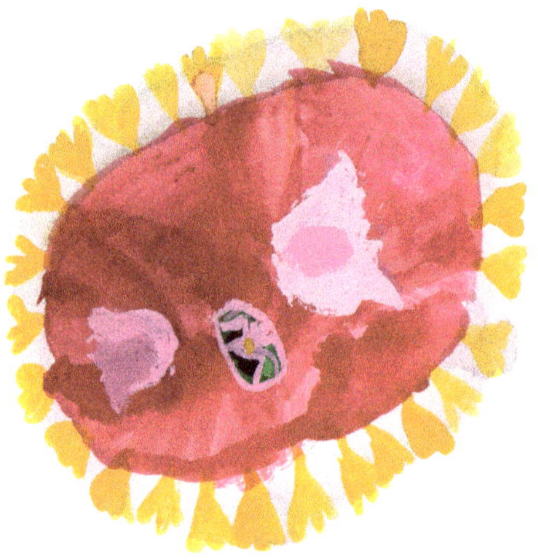

Megan Gollaher, *Cat Flower,* watercolor and gouache

Inspired when she looked at a draft of this book,
my 7-year-old granddaughter painted a mandala for me
and asked that I include it in the book. This is a mandala of
flowers, some of which are hearts. What a gift!

"In art the hand can never execute anything higher than the heart can inspire." —Ralph Waldo Emerson

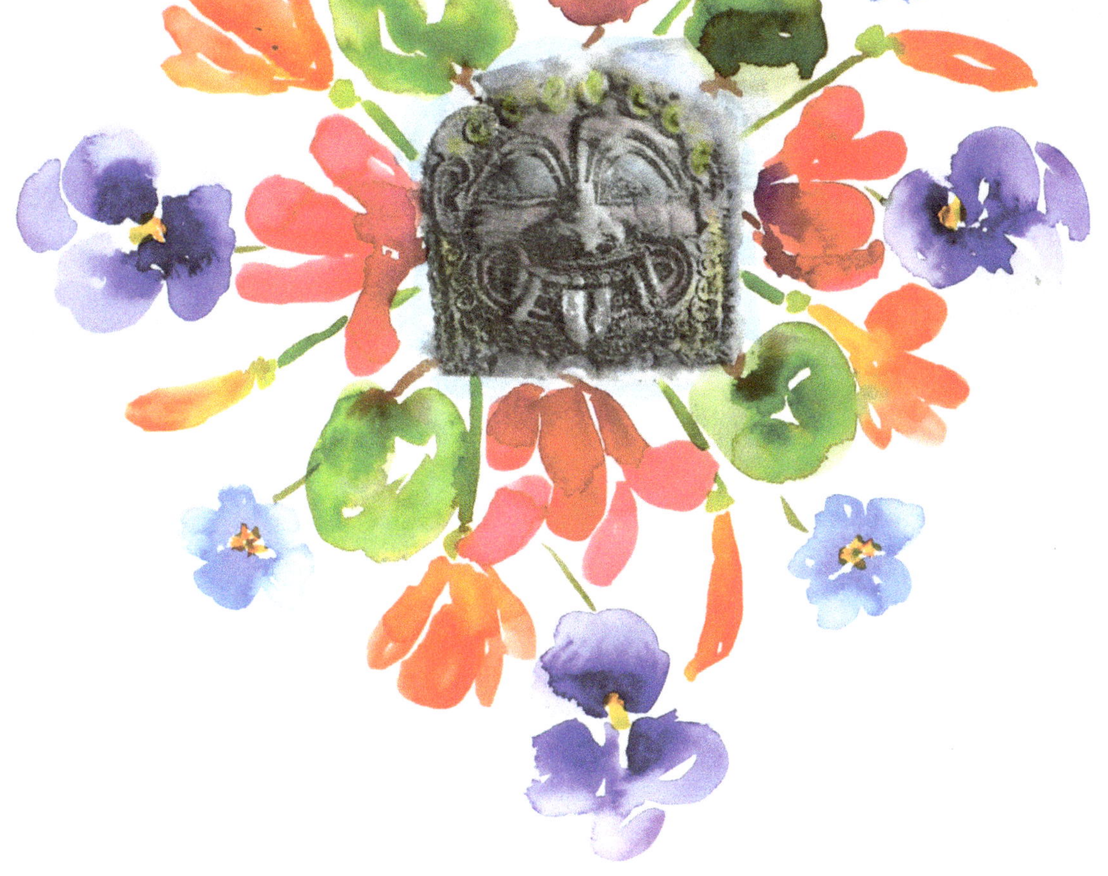

CHAPTER EIGHT

Embracing The Shadow

What's In The Darkness?

"Do you ever paint your darkness?" an elderly woman asked me when I showed her some of my flower paintings. Truthfully, I'd never thought of it. I was content to paint flowers, had yet to discover mandalas, and kept my "inner paintings" well hidden. Like a lot of us, looking at our dark side, let alone committing it to paint and paper, was not such an appealing idea. My old friend had planted a thought. What *would* I paint if I were to paint my darkness, and why had I never wanted to?

I thought about that for a long time, and eventually I did paint the darkness. See *Do You Ever Paint Your Darkness?* The circle and square motif in this mandala is called the "squaring of the circle," and is not uncommon in traditional mandalas. It creates a "balancing of opposites."[1] It was exactly what I needed at the time. According to Jung, there is a tension created by the struggle between the conscious and unconscious when our personal shadow starts to become conscious. A mandala will spontaneously arise in the mind "as a representation of the struggle and reconciliation of opposites. It is felt as 'grace.'"[2]

Experiencing that grace is what we're after in this phase of our mandala work. That sounds nice, but there is often apprehension in approaching our shadow. There was for me, and there certainly was for students in my classes. Most everyone gets nervous about this process, and yet, I consistently found that some of the richest mandalas were ones in which the intention was to become aware of the shadow. One student who had done a lot of mandala work announced to all of us in class one day, "You can't get away from it—the shadow is always in *every* mandala." So why is that?

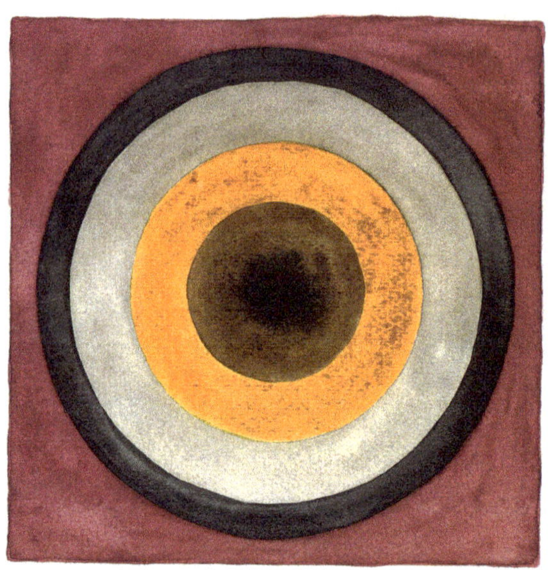

Do You Ever Paint Your Darkness? Watercolor

These somber target-like circles hovered over me for days and I tried to ignore them because they were unfamiliar and uncomfortable. When they appeared in a dream I knew they wouldn't go away until I painted them. In the dream the circles were surrounded by the dark red square which made me feel more settled about painting them. I have come to really like this mandala.

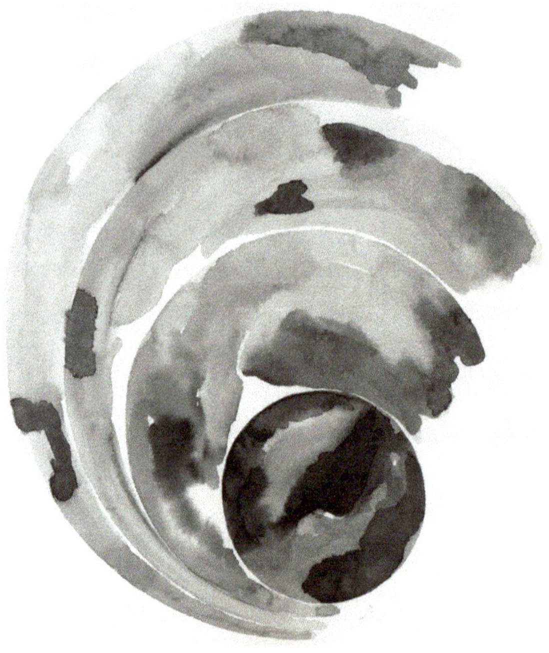

Sara Fisher-Smith, *Fear,* watercolor

Fear surrounds/Distorts/In mirky darkness/It moves out/Hopeful To enlist another/Loses its momentum/Then/Dissipates
—Sara Fisher-Smith

What Is The "Shadow?"

As defined in Jungian terms the shadow is "an unconscious part of the personality characterized by traits and attitudes, whether negative or positive, which the conscious ego tends to reject or ignore. Consciously assimilating one's shadow usually results in an increase of energy."[3] To make it even simpler, Jung is reported to have told a group of therapists who were nit-picking over the exact definition of the shadow, "The shadow is simply the whole unconscious."[4] Like our actual human shadow, it's a part of ourselves we often don't see or focus on, and, in itself is neither negative or positive. So, why do we want to look at it in mandalas? Because our journey is to become whole, and whole means the entirety—*the whole enchilada*. And, with the possibility of an increase in energy, I'll go for that!

I like what Robert Bly says in his book *A Little Book on the Human Shadow*. Our personal shadow is the "long bag we drag behind us" into which we put parts of ourselves which we thought others didn't like. "We spend our life until we're twenty deciding what parts of ourselves to put into the bag, and we spend the rest of our lives trying to get them out again...."[5] The more we stuff in the bag, he says, the more energy gets stuffed along with it, leaving us with a bag full of inaccessible energy and pieces of ourselves. In our life if we have felt non-creative and unartistic, the reason according to Bly, is that our creativity has simply been hidden in the bag where we shoved it. We put it there when we thought, or were told, someone didn't like it.

Retrieving Our Shadow

The big question, of course, is how do we retrieve our shadow or those parts of ourselves that we've stuffed away? How do we get our energy back? Or our creativity? Try painting the shadow Bly says. "When we paint the witch (our shadow) with conscious intention, we soon find out whose house she's in—where we've put it."[6] The shadow is often projected on others and we need to realize that this projection is really about ourselves. Sara Fisher-Smith's *Fear* is a very graphic example of projection, especially with the use of black and white. "If the ancients were right that darkness contains intelligence and nourishment and even information, then the person who eats his or her own shadow is more energetic as well as more intelligent."[7]

Stuffing, projecting and painting the witch is not unfamiliar to me. Years ago, I went to a dream painting workshop with a soon-to-be ex-boyfriend, who, not so incidentally, was an artist and married to his work. No longer able to contain my unhappiness about our relationship, a "witch woman" exploded in poster paint on my paper. She dripped blood and had orange-colored snakes for hair and black, armor-plated breasts. Empowered following the workshop experience, I finally ended the old, unworkable relationship. I brought my own paintings out from their hiding place under my bed and took back my projected creativity. I had been what *The Artist's Way* calls a "shadow artist," dating someone who pursued the art career I secretly longed for because I was unable to recognize my own creativity.[8] I told a man at work, a graphic designer with whom I had become good friends, about my painting and he asked to see it. When I showed it to him, to my astonishment, he liked it and offered to buy it. I couldn't imagine letting someone else have my witch, but his enthusiasm kept me from throwing her away. I rolled her up into a big yellow map tube and stuck her in my closet. Eventually I married the designer, and the witch woman became part of our garaged stuff. She remained there for many years, until she reappeared to me in a bodywork session. I came home and said, "Honey, let's find my witch woman." We let her out of the tube

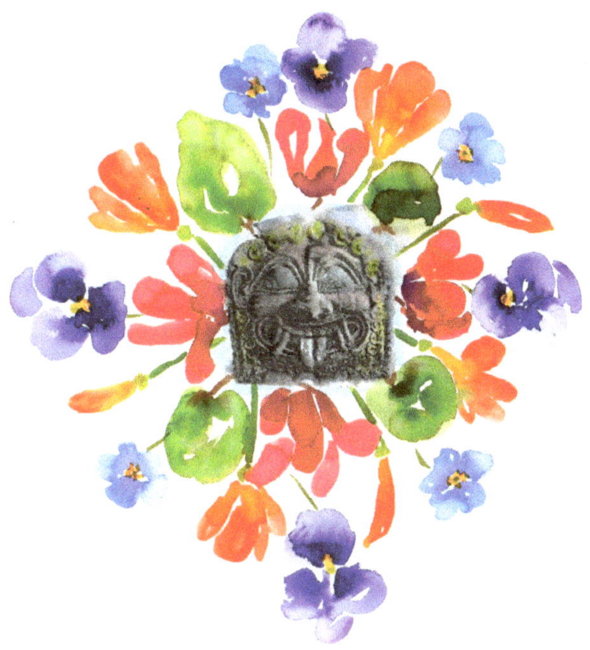

Sometimes I Feel Like Medusa, watercolor, ink transfer

My witch energy has always been a challenge for me to own. My intention for this mandala was to acknowledge it.

and she really did look beautiful—to both of us. My husband thinks she is one of the most spontaneous and bold things I've ever done, and still wants to have her framed. "So you'll remember the energy," he says. Maybe that's not such a bad idea. Sometime later, when my witch inevitably surfaced again, I sat with her in the garden and painted her surrounded with flowers. She is the centerpiece of the mandala above, *Sometimes I Feel Like Medusa*.

TIBETAN AND NAVAHO MANDALAS

This projecting and reabsorbing the projection of our shadow, is not unlike the way of life of the Navajo and Tibetan native described in *Sacred Wisdom: The Circle of Spirit*. For these natives "life is a process of constant rebalancing and perfecting of one's actions, expressions, and thoughts into an ideal state...."[9] For the Navajo, this state is called "Beauty."[10] In order to become enlightened, according to their beliefs, one must purify unen-

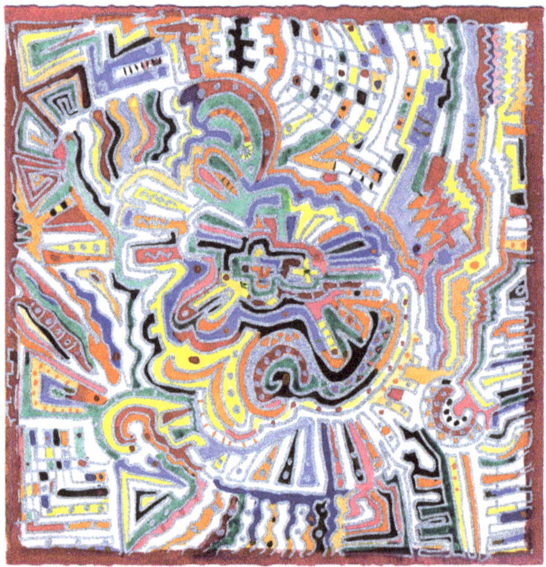

Steve Schulz, *Untitled*, watercolor, silver felt pen

Steve was always trying something new and it was inspirational watching him create new techniques. Here he was fascinated with how the felt pen, which he applied first, resisted the watercolor.

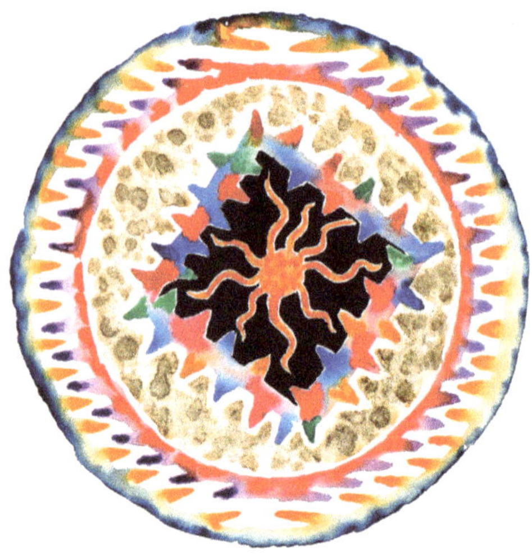

John McCaffrey, *The Inner Sun*, watercolor, gold ink

The inner Sun shines in pure Eternity.
Beyond all thoughts...
Senses...time...
Or even space.

–John McCaffrey

lightened and distorted thinking called "poisons." The poisons of anger, pride, lust, jealousy and ignorance, when transformed, become enlightened wisdom and powerful energies on the spiritual path.[11] It sounds like the ultimate in spiritual recycling! The shadow is welcomed and, in fact, needed. Energies of a lower nature are used to develop higher energies. All parts of the self are used, nothing is dismissed. See how Steve Schulz depicts that in his amazing mandala, *Untitled*.

For the Tibetans and the Navaho the mandala is the expression of this spiritual path of transformation. Their mandalas often will show the journey of a spiritual hero moving toward the still point within the center, the place of enlightenment and peace. The seeker becomes transformed in the process of moving toward this center. In my mandala on page 56, *Light Penetrates the Pool of Wonder*, the dark energies are transformed by the light moving toward the center.

The quest for "grace," or the center, is the pivotal point of our mandala work. The shadow is an absolutely essential part of the journey. It is like the Eastern Indian Upanishads metaphor of a shadowy spider sitting at the center of its web. The spider issues and reabsorbs its threads in concentric circles, and all the threads can be traced back to the central point of the web. This apparently simple metaphor shows the essence of Indian thought: "Awakening ones inner centre implies gathering one's self into a single creative point and integrating and balancing its expansion into a totality. To centre one's self is essentially a way toward inner awakening."[12] See the beautiful spidery image in John McCaffrey's mandala *The Inner Sun*.

MYSTERIOUS AND POWERFUL

The acknowledgement of the shadow can be quite mysterious and powerful. An image of an artichoke heart kept coming to mind in the early hours one morning when I couldn't sleep. It seemed insistent, and I knew that I needed to paint it, but why I did not know. So the next morning I began work on a big, bright, colorful cross-section of an artichoke heart. As I painted, a former friend-turned-landord popped into my mind. She had moved out of town and we had not spoken in over ten years because of an old misunderstanding. I felt it was now time to heal that. So, in the middle of this painting, I picked up the phone, got her number from long distance information and called. She answered, remarkable in itself. I said it was time to break our silence, and asked her forgiveness for my part in our old disagreement. Surprised and excited, she said, "I've read about people doing this in Ann Lander's column!" After a pleasant conversation and a mended friendship, I went back to painting the artichoke. But, over and over in my mind I kept repeating like a mantra, "Deep in the heart of the artichoke, deep in the heart of the artichoke." And then I really heard it, "Deep in the heart of the art I choke." This wasn't about artichokes! It was about what was buried deep in my heart, choking my art. For me that was old resentments. It became clear that as I painted *Deep In The Heart Of The Art-I-Choke* I was pulling something very old out of my bag.

"If we can learn to forgive those we believe betrayed us, we can call our spirits back into present time," says Carolyn Myss, leader of workshops on why people don't heal. "Through this act, we can heal emotionally, and have more energy available to heal physically." [13]

LETTING GO OF OLD WOUNDS

As I was completing this chapter I came face to face with a huge piece of my shadow. What synchronicity. I ran into my old high school art teacher who had given me a "D" in a design class in high school when my course work did not

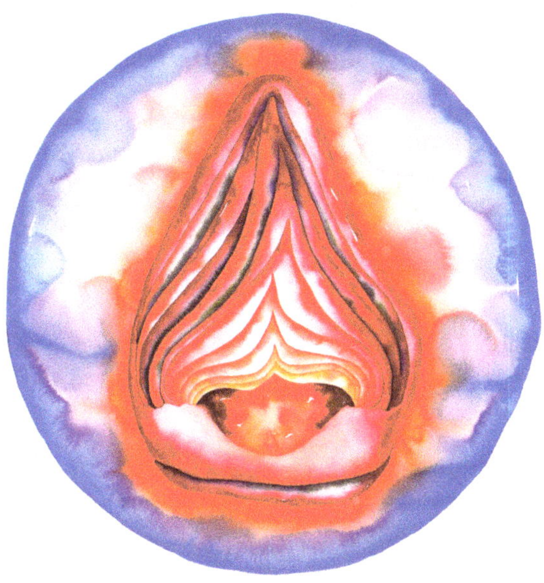

Deep In The Heart Of The Art-I-Choke, watercolor

The energy that was released when I painted this and realized its meaning was tremendous. The process involved with this mandala was one of the most powerful I had ever experienced.

warrant it. I did not understand! It was the worst grade I had ever gotten in any subject—let alone art, and it crushed me. It became my favorite "poor-me" story about hurtful art teachers and I got a lot of mileage out of it when I told it—which I did for years. I believed he was responsible for me feeling completely incapable of doing art, and because of that, I pursued art history, studying *about* art rather than doing it. Finally, I knew it was time to let go of that story when I realized it had become easier to blame my teacher than to muster the courage to do my art. So running into him that day in the supermarket, became my opportunity. "Give yourself the dignity of admitting your artistic wounds," says Julia Cameron in *The Artist's Way*. "That is the first step in healing them." [14] I told him how bad I had felt in his class years ago, and how the awful grade had affected me for a long time. He sincerely apologized. I then got to tell him that I had become an artist and with that we seemed to become equals. What a relief to finally let go of the anger I held toward him and what renewed energy it brought me.

How To Paint A Shadow Mandala

BEGIN BY SETTING YOUR INTENTION and write it on the back of your paper. This can seem a little scary at first, but in my experience, the shadow mandala can be full of such wealth. Don't try to come up with an idea of your shadow before you begin. Let the light illuminate it. Be gentle with yourself. Of course, you may know some part of your shadow you'd like to work on, and you can set that intention accordingly. Otherwise, you can say "I intend to co-create with spirit having fun or enjoying myself in the process of acknowledging my shadow." Or, write it in any way that is comfortable for you. For the shadow mandala especially, that is important. Go into meditation, bring your intention into your heart, and chant OM. Observe what happens, even if it doesn't make sense right off. "What a watermelon!" a student once said, as she came out of the meditation rather perplexed. And, painting it turned out to have a very profound meaning for her.

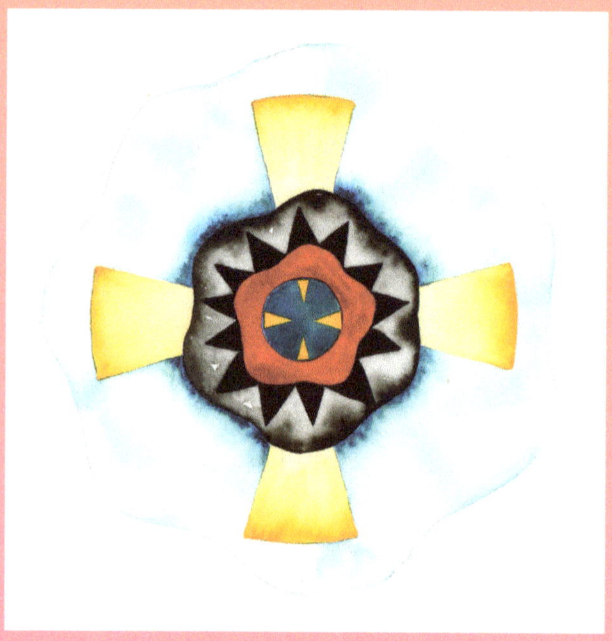

Light Penetrates The Pool Of Wonder, watercolor

The black wall of doubt and torment tries to keep
the light out, but the light penetrates and prevails.

"We do not become enlightened by imagining figures of light, but by making the darkness conscious." –Carl Jung

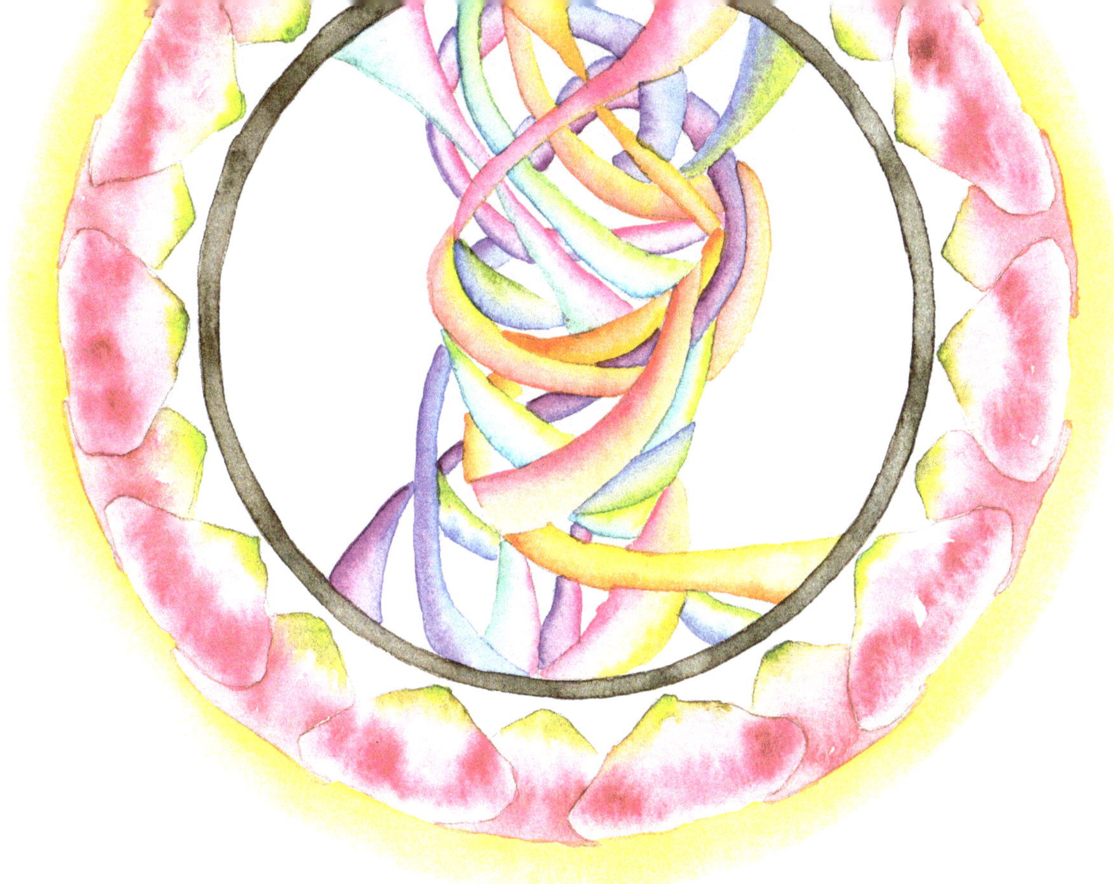

THE HEALING POWER OF MANDALAS

A MEANINGFUL EXPERIENCE

With this chapter we are entering the final segment of what was originally a 6-week class. I have expanded the book to 9 chapters which, I believe, will allow for better assimilation of all that has been presented. It is for healing that many of us have been drawn to the mandala experience. When you try one, know you will be wonderfully rewarded. In painting a healing mandala some will say that we've saved the best until last. In some ways that is true, because the healing mandala is a very, very special one.

Each mandala has its rewards and challenges. Most find the first quick mandala easy and freeing, emotion mandalas calming and balancing, the flower mandala fascinating, and the seed mandala imaginative and creative. In the inner child mandala we usually get the most playful, and in the shadow mandala we find a wealth of undiscovered riches. And, once we have painted any of the mandalas, we soon see that *all* mandalas are healing in some way. But, the healing mandala is unique in itself. What I've noticed is that it's the healing mandala which will offer deeper insights, sometimes revealing more questions than answers. I have experienced healing images which appear to boggle the mind, change as they are being painted, and seem not to make any sense at all. To paint a healing mandala, that is, to have the intent in a mandala to heal some part of our life, whether it be our body, mind, emotions, spirit, our relationships, our life's work, or the planet, and, to ask for and co-create a healing image, is a deeply meaningful experience.

WHAT IS THE GOAL OF HEALING?

In his autobiography Carl Jung tells us what it is from his experience. While working on mandalas himself he wrote: "The question arose repeatedly: Where is this process leading to? Where is its goal? I saw that everything, all the paths I had been following, all the steps I had taken, were leading back to a single point....It became increasingly plain to me that the mandala is the center. It is the exponent of all paths. It is the path to the center...the goal is the self. There is no linear evolution; there is only a circumambulation of the self....The self is the principle and archetype of orientation and meaning. Therein lies its healing function."[1]

All roads lead back to the center. The center, or the self, is the origin, the place from which all else arises. It is the pattern from which all else is based. It is the place from which all evolves, and to which all returns. It is where disease can be transformed into ease, where ignorance can be transformed into wisdom, where darkness turns into light and fear dissolves into love. It is the unknowable and unnameable. It is found in the center of ourselves. It is that which gives us orientation and gives us meaning. It is the spirit within. This center, Jung says, " is the goal."

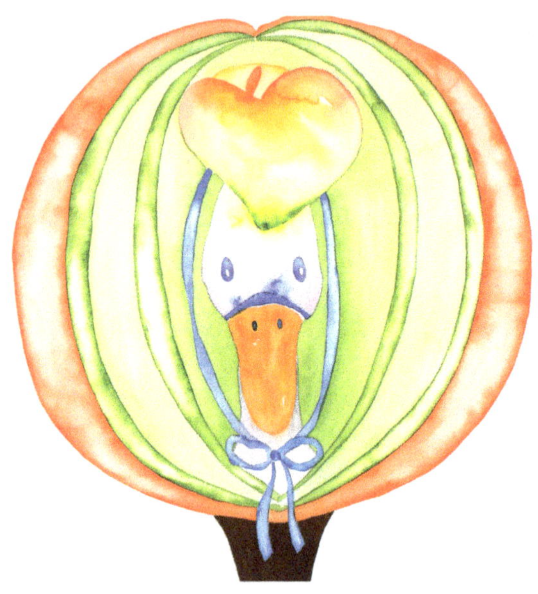

There Is An Answer, watercolor, gold ink

This image was not what I was expecting, nor was it what I saw in meditation, but the message it brought me was very profound.

MY COMMITMENT TO HEALING

One very surprising and delightful mandala I created came at the culmination of a series I had been painting for the healing of Chronic Fatigue Syndrome. Having been to many, many doctors and practitioners over a 10-year period, none of whom could find what was the matter, my friend Lane Cara Shaw recommended her son who was an internist. He specialized, coincidently, in treating chronic conditions such as this and used integrated medicine, a combination of Eastern and Western. When he diagnosed me with CFS, I made a commitment to myself and to him to do my part to heal my disease through my mandalas. Practically every painting I did for about 6 months was intended to provide answers, insight and direction for my healing.

My health began to improve considerably, from the herbs and supplements I started taking, a special diet and from the mandalas I painted. These mandalas were quite interesting, and what I observed in the process, was that I was becoming more free, open and spontaneous.

"THERE IS AN ANSWER"

One hard day toward the end of this period of focused intent, I asked in frustration in meditation, "Will this ever end?" I heard, "There is an answer," and saw a simple silhouette of a white swan and a calla lily. I thought that it would be a fairly easy image to do, and figured I'd paint it during class while everyone else worked. So much for those plans. As I started drawing the swan, I got nervous, almost panicked and thought, "I don't know how to draw a swan, how do you do it?" What I was drawing was becoming a goose, and, of course, I wanted to stop right there and not embarrass myself any further in front of everyone. "This isn't right," my inner critic declared. And another voice said, "Keep going and trust the process, just like you tell everyone else to do." Darn.

Here I was, knowing I needed to trust the process, but being faced with those old feelings of being inadequate, incapable and afraid of making a mistake. I noticed that I was sweating, but I kept going. Then the calla lily landed on the goose's head and became a hat. "This is ridiculous!" I thought. It looked like Mother Goose, which you can see on the previous page in *There Is An Answer.* I was confused, although I did start to laugh at this silly goose looking at me lovingly from the paper, and which everyone else in the class seemed to see before I did. I took it home and finished it, and just accepted that my swan was Mother Goose. "Actually," I mused, "How nice it would be to be loved by a Mother Goose as loving as this." My husband seemed to have no problem with its meaning. "It's you," he said. "It's how you 'Mother Goose' everyone." He had been telling me for years that I spent too much time taking care of others to the detriment of myself, which he called "Mother Goosing." Dr. Shaw confirmed it—people with CFS are usually those who have habitually put others before themselves, and have worn themselves out by doing so. There was the answer! I'm sure there's even more to it. For starters, maybe I was being told to lighten up and not take myself, nor the mandalas, so seriously.

THE FEAR IN MANDALAS

In all honesty, once I got passed the fear, I really enjoyed doing the Mother Goose mandala and being part of the humorous process. Letting go, trusting and walking through the fear isn't exactly a piece of cake for any of us, but, how interesting the journey and how glad we are when we are on the other side of it. I happen to be one of those people who doesn't like fear, or being out of control or in pain. Well, who does? But, here's something I have learned. I'm not sure there is any mandala that *isn't* without fear, somewhere. Because, that *is* the process.

Energetic healer Barbara Brennan, in her book *Hands of Light*, talks about healing and fear:

"Any illness you have is a direct result of the fact that you have not fully followed what you wish to do. How have you not harkened to that inner voice. How have you not let yourself be fully who you are? Any illness is a direct message to you that tells you (that) you have not been loving who you are, cherishing yourself in order to be who you are. *This is the basis of all healing.*

"And so, having found the answer, you will immediately find, most likely, *pain* and *fear* where you have blocked yourself from doing what you have really desired to do. And at that point, the choice is to face the fear and allow yourself to feel it and to work with it in your life. For whenever there is fear, there has been then the absence of love, for fear is the opposite of love. For wherever there is fear, you can be sure you are not in truth....You are not centered, you are not within the wholeness of your being when you are afraid.

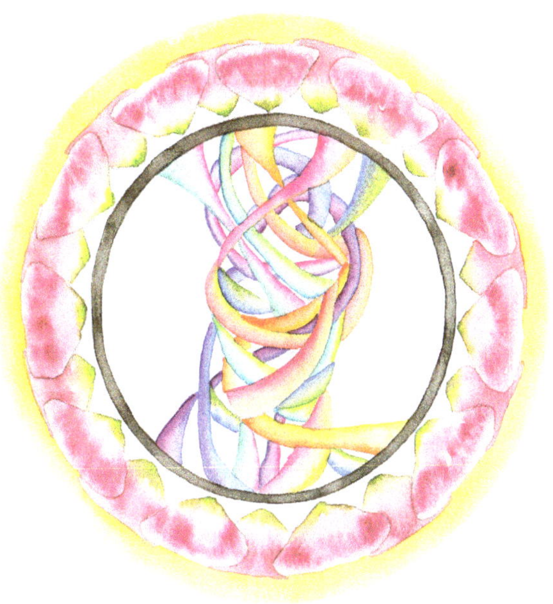

All Tangled Up, watercolor

This image of tangled up pastel vines had been with me for a few days. Stepping into the feelings, I painted this mandala for the healing of fear and anxiety.

When you take courage to step into the fear, you begin the healing process on a new level."[2]

HOW WE DO LIFE IS HOW WE PAINT

Don't let anyone tell you there isn't some fear in doing mandalas. I keep hoping that one day I won't have it anymore, that it will go away for good. However, I also know the elation of walking through fear, of conquering it. You just can't beat how good it feels. *All Tangled Up* represents being tied in knots internally. Healing came as the fear was faced. It released into soft flower petals.

For a long time I have noticed that doing my art is no different than doing my life. I face the same fears, the same frustrations, it's just the medium that's different. I get angry and afraid when I can't do something perfectly right-off, whether in paint on paper or in my life. We all bump into ourselves wherever we go. Life is our mirror. It's not going to be any different in our mandalas, for it turns out that how we do life is how we paint. That's the truth. And, it's a good thing. We don't have to keep avoiding ourselves. We'll find ourselves fast enough in the mandalas.

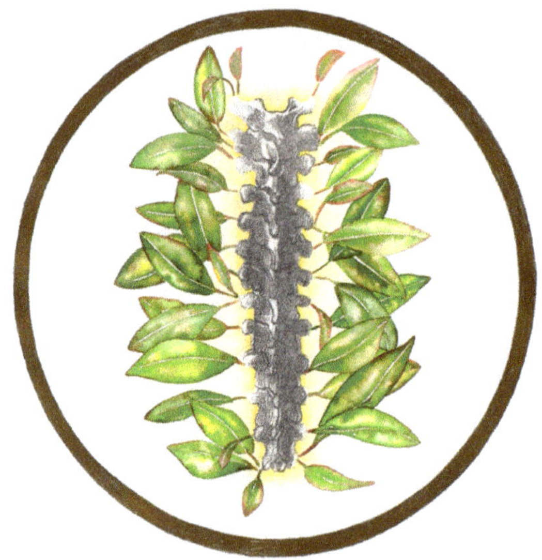

The Nature of Myself, watercolor, ink transfer

This image came in meditation. Light and energy flowed up my spine and my spine sprouted leaves.

WHAT ARE YOU DOING ABOUT YOUR CREATIVITY?

I'm healthier than I've been in a long time. I am healing. And I'm healing because I'm doing more and more of what I love, my creative expression. Several years ago one practitioner asked me in an initial visit, "And, what are you doing about your creativity?" I thought, "What's *that* got to do with my healing?" Well I learned it had *everything* to do with it! I love how Barbara Brennan put it: "Healing turns into creativity as one moves into the light and holds it within. As the darkness fades, the transformation process becomes one of creativity rather than of healing." [3]

IS PAINTING MANDALAS HEALING?

Do I believe that painting mandalas is healing? Yes, I do. But what stumped me for a long time was *why*. Why exactly are mandalas healing? I could see the process working on me for years, but I wanted that definitive reason. Putting that intention out, the answer came while taking *The Painting Experience* workshop in San Francisco. I was not feeling well at all the day I went to the workshop and really had wanted to cancel. It was too late to get my money back. I decided to go anyway, and do the best that I could, even if it meant that all I would do was sit in a heap like a slug and dab paint on the paper. I told the facilitator that I was just too tired to paint. She told me to go ahead and do just a little of whatever would make me happy and to simply observe my energy as I did that. So, of course, the more I did what I wanted with no expectation from anyone, the more surprisingly energized I felt. When my energy would drop, we'd check it out, and it was always from doing what I thought I should or what I thought would look good. This up and down shifting of energy happened all day, and by the end of the day I got it. I was energized when I followed where my energy wanted to go, where it made me happy. I got tired when I had expectations and struggled too hard to make things work.

BEING IN THE FLOW

I have continued to watch and follow my energy as I do my mandalas and it has been invaluable in understanding the healing power of this work. I have always known that I must follow my truth. I say that repeatedly to myself and to others in class. But, I think it really took getting sick to fully understand how that worked in my own life. That was how I got the answer I'd been looking for. Painting is touching the creative spark of life, the flow and movement of all life. Being in the flow of this creative energy is enlivening, it brings life and healing through us as seen symbolically in my mandala on page 60, *The Nature of My Self.*

In order to keep that flow going when I paint, I'll ask, especially if I feel unsure as to what to do next, "Where does the energy want to go, what would be fun and where do I want to go?" I have to catch myself if I ask, "Where do I *think* I should go." This is usually connected to what others will think or what *I* think others will think. What will give me joy? Truth? Energy? And, what must be expressed *now*?

THE GREATEST GIFT

Watch how exciting it is to paint whatever you want, however you want, and with no judgements from anyone, most of all yourself. Your truth will flow through your hand, I promise you, for it cannot do otherwise. And you will sing your own song in your brush strokes. And, they will be yours alone. Allowing and accepting them as your own beautiful marks is sometimes harder

than creating. Creating is natural. Our High Self really does desire to create, to make our marks, to sing our song, to let the energy of the universe flow through us, uninhibited, and to express this energy in our own unique way. Can you see how blocking that would just stop up the works and cause disease? It's the ultimate creative act, this channeling of divine energy. Get out of its way, with your judgements and hesitations and small mind chatter. Honor it, and it will honor you, love it and it will love you, but don't walk away. This is really the greatest gift you can give yourself, to flow with the energy of your divine self and let it show you who you really are.

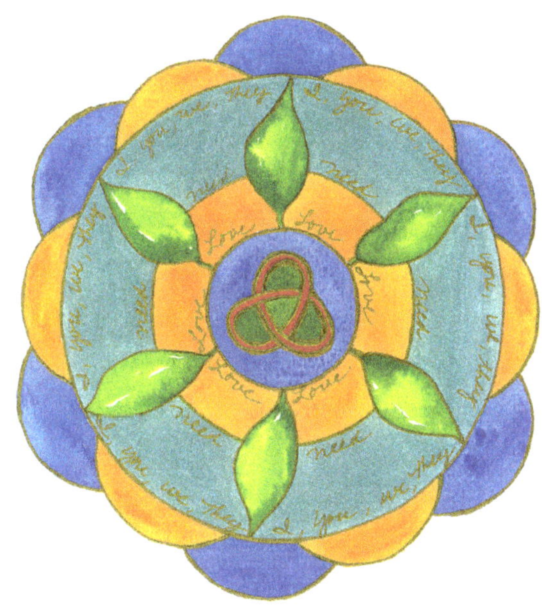

I, You, We, They Need Love, watercolor, gold felt pen

When we wish to move beyond our personal healing, we can offer good thoughts for the healing of others and the healing of the planet. I painted this mandala for those who suffered during rioting in Southern California after the Rodney King trial. Because I could not be there, it felt like it was something I *could* do. I learned later that the image in the center is an eternal love knot.

How To Get Started On A Healing Mandala

DECIDE WHAT SORT OF HEALING you wish to focus on in a mandala. Is it a physical problem, or an emotional one, or perhaps a relationship? Maybe it's simply "healing" in general. I have often written just that as my intention. Write your intention on the back of your watercolor paper. " I intend to co-create with spirit a healing mandala for insight, answers and direction on my current issue," for example. Relax, go into meditation, bring your intention into your heart, and chant the OM chant. Watch and listen for whatever images, or stirrings you receive. Do not reject any of them, however odd or seemingly unrelated they may be.

Honor whatever comes, for it will in some way have a piece or pieces of your answer. And, if you do not understand your mandala after you paint it, or you want further information, then you may want to do another, with a more specific intention. If that is the case try, "What is the very next step in my healing process?" Or perhaps an even more gentle approach would bring up the helpful answers and energies you're needing, "I intend to have fun and do the best I can do in my healing mandala." It is important never to push aside what comes—it is always part of the treasure, your treasure. Don't reject what may be the next piece of the puzzle, however tempting it may be to do so, or unimportant it may seem!

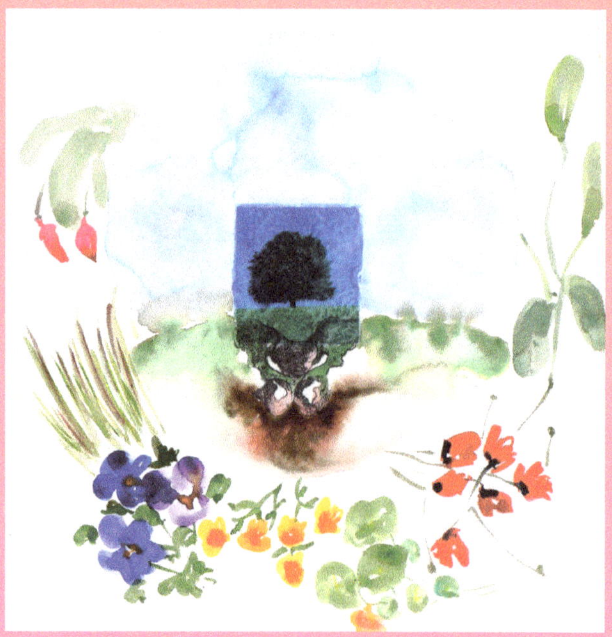

Please Receive My Suffering, watercolor, ink transfer

I saw the image of a pelvis releasing into the ground, as Native Americans had done, the suffering of my great-grandmothers, my grandmothers and my mother. This came to me in a bodywork session as I was releasing the suffering of these women which I carried in my body. Where the blood was released, the earth was nourished and flowers grew. This was the first time I used the ink transfer process with photocopies (pelvic bone and tree) which was so much fun and opened up a future of new possibilities.

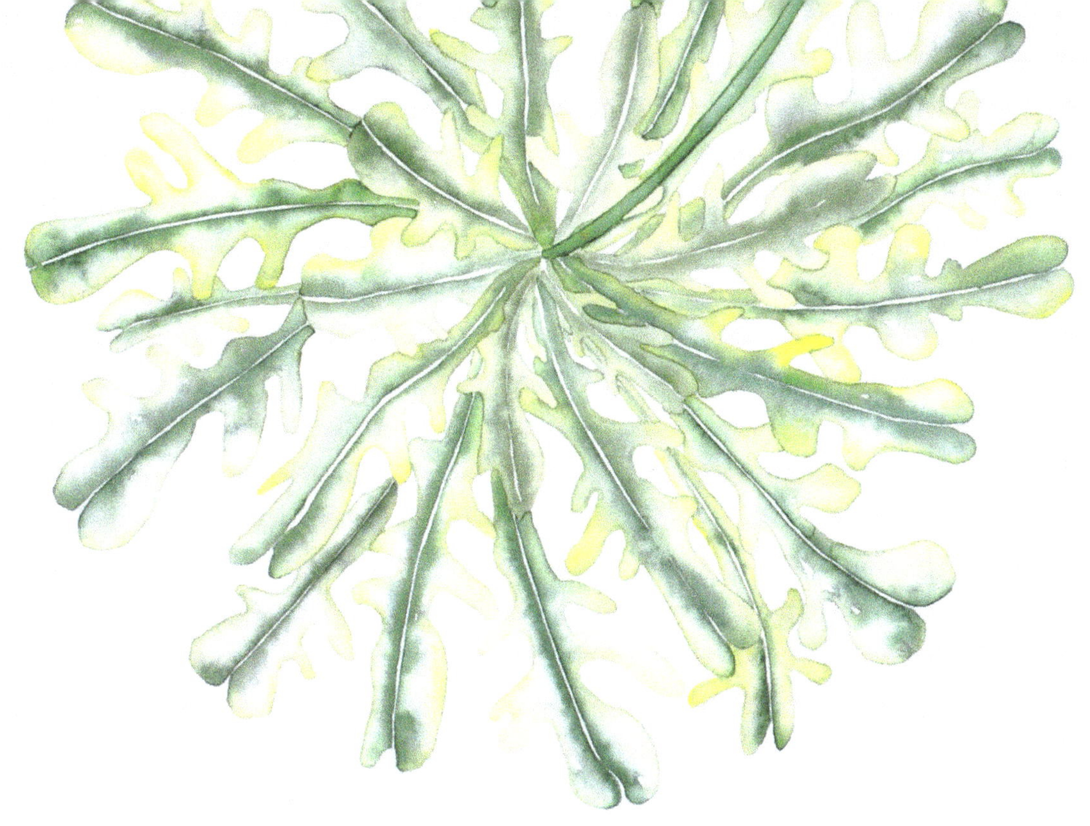

A New-Found Inner Treasure

How It Started

Art In My Heart really started from my secret heart drawings and paintings. That morning in 1978, while trying to wake up and face my day as a public relations director, I saw a vision of my heart rising up over green hills like the sun. It dawned a new day in my life and became a very personal symbol for an inner awakening I was beginning to experience. I *happened* to read later that evening in Carl Jung's *Memories, Dreams and Reflections*, "There is no better means of intensifying the treasured feeling of individuality than the possession of a secret which the individual is pledged to guard."[1]

Yes, I was in possession of a secret. Kept hidden from others, my inner heart paintings touched such a deep core of joy, power and truth in me that I was truly in awe. I was discovering that I *could* paint, and when I painted from my heart and about my heart, it gave me one of the greatest inner satisfactions I had ever known. Jung's term "secret" was perfect. Like a child who is delighted beyond description, *My Secret*, page 4, represented the beginning of the discovery of my new-found inner treasure.

I was no longer interested in painting the traditional watercolor landscapes I had been taught in school and I was also becoming increasingly disinterested in the business world. So I ventured into a journey of my own inner landscape looking for the secret of the heart. I think finding the mandala was inevitable for me on this inward path. Eventually, I had to find the center, the starting point, the origin. I don't believe I knew where I'd end up, or that I was heading anywhere in particular. I just kept going, rather blindly as I see it now. Not knowing what to expect at the center, it surprised me when I physically stumbled onto it.

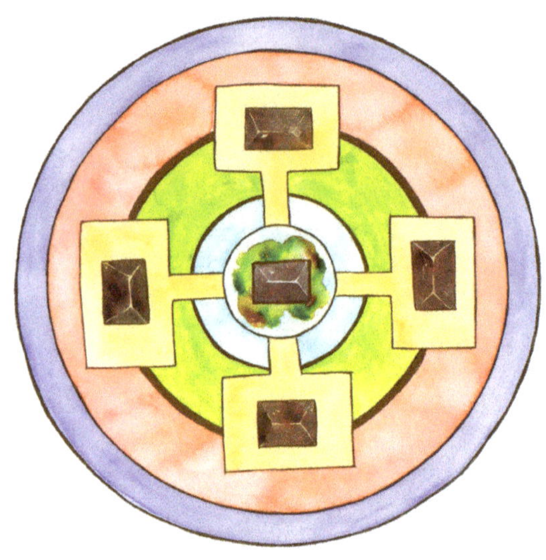

The Dream Of Ranch House Circle,
watercolor, gold felt pen

In painting the experience of visiting my grandparents old ranch house, I loosely used the format of a traditional Tibetan mandala. Generally an architectural palace-like structure, they are surrounded by a ring of fire for purification. Gateways representing aspects of the lower nature which are to be transformed, lead to the center from the four points of the compass. My mandala is representative of the same movement and goal as ancient mandalas—consciousness, awakening to who we really are. The center is the goal, which represents enlightenment.

A TRIP TO THE PAST

I came to the center when I took a trip back to my grandparent's house after they had been dead for about 40 years. I had had a dream that their dairy farm and peach orchard had been developed into a housing subdivision, but their old ranch house remained intact in the middle of it all. Ten years later I went to see the old house after I had the dream again. When I got there, I made my way through a maze of new houses by sighting a tall sycamore tree from the main road, the one I played under as a child. The tree, as in the dreams, was in the center, next to the old house. The house was remodeled but on its original foundation, and in the middle of the new cul-de-sac called Ranch House Circle. I stood under the tree and was immediately struck by the smell of the same grass and tree bark. The memories were powerful and jarred me, but were good. Not wanting to cause too much suspicion, nor wanting to engage with anyone, I peeled a piece of bark from the old tree and left.

As I drove away I was surprised by angry feelings which surfaced. Underneath those, however, was a deep, powerful love which I felt was trying to find its way up for some air. I had been so loved and cherished by my grandparents and had been completely secure in that love. I began to realize I had been brought back to this place to connect with that. Because I had been so shattered and confused by their sudden deaths, I had buried away those feelings of love. I was 6-years-old when they both died, two months apart, of brain cancer. I realized that, as a child, I had built a protective wall of toughness and anger around myself to survive the pain of their loss.

In returning to this place I was facing the origin of my old anger and grief. And, as I faced it, I began to remember that what was on the inside of me was love—old, deep love. I was like the old house. My foundation remained, covered with new growth, but, in tact and still there, nonetheless. I had traveled a long way in 40 years to find my center. As T. S. Eliot once wrote, "We shall not cease from exploration, and the end of all exploring will be to arrive where we started and know the place for the first time." [2]

I painted the above mandala after the visit and reconnection to my grandparents' house. The lavender is the color my grandmother loved to wear, the peach color from the peach orchards, the green from the pastures, the blue of the skies, the green sycamore tree under which I used to play and the old house at the center. It was a wonderful experience.

"Sometimes one must travel far to discover what is near."
–Uri Shulevitz

MANDALAS REPRESENT OUR SPIRITUAL JOURNEY

"Because the Power of the World always works in circles," said Black Elk, "Everything tries to be round."[3] We have come full circle, understanding that mandalas represent a spiritual journey of our own. We have made this journey through the practice and process of learning to paint mandalas. And what a wonderful tale we have woven as we traveled, painting our colorful light and energy. We have told our stories. We have explored ourselves through mandalas from every angle, from what's in front of us, to what's behind, and what's on the right of us and on the left. We have committed ourselves to go beyond our mind, beyond our ego and to travel to the truth of our self.

We have taken this journey by asking for help from the Light, and have let go and trusted that we could consciously co-create in this way. We have begun to let go of our self-judgments about our creative abilities and are learning that by practice we are growing beyond yesterday and forward into tomorrow. We are learning to have fun with it all and not take ourselves so seriously. We are enjoying our journey of self-discovery and opening up to the incredibly rich and infinite world of our inner self. We are learning to flow and flower with the creative universal energy. We are planting seeds of self love, healing and embracing all parts of ourselves. Many of us will have found our way to our center to realize what is there is love. And, that who we are is love.

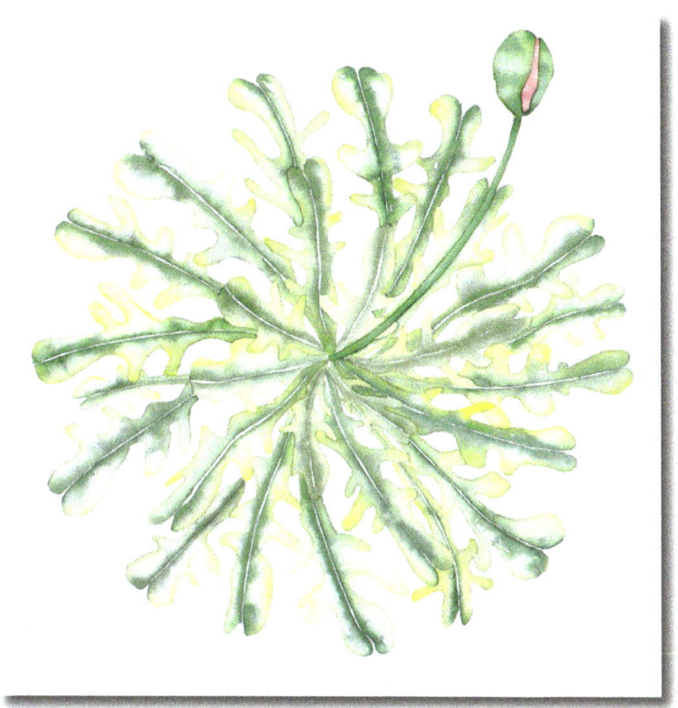

This Bud's For You, watercolor

We have come full circle, learning to flower in the light,
have fun and not take ourselves so seriously.

DEDICATION PAGE, INTRODUCTION

1. Seiler, Eddie. Marcus, Sol. Benjamin, Bennie. Durham, Eddie. "I Don't Want to Set the World on Fire." *Cherio Music Pub.* N.Y.C. 1941.

2. Tenzin-Dolma, Lisa. *Natural Mandalas.* Duncan Baird Pub. London. 2006. Pg. 11.

3. *The Spiritual in Art 1890-1985.* Los Angeles Museum of Art. Abbeville Press. 1986. Pg. 375.

4. Arguelles, Jose & Miriam. *Mandala.* Shambala Publications. Boulder & London. 1972. Pg. 13.

CHAPTER TWO

1. Butler, Ram. *Siddha Yoga Correspondence Course.* N.Y. 1994. Lesson 27. Pg. 4.

2. Goldsmith, Joel S. *The Art of Meditation.* Harper & Row. N.Y. 1956. Pgs. 10-13.

CHAPTER THREE

1. Jung, Carl, ed. *Man and His Symbols.* Dell. N.Y. 1971. Pg. 231.

2. Jung, Carl. *Memories, Dreams, Reflections.* Ed. Aneila Jaffe. Trans. Richard & Clara Winston. Vintage Books. N. Y. 1965. Pgs. 195-197.

3. Ibid. Pg. 177.

CHAPTER FOUR

1. Naylor, Hope. *Rainbows Are For Everybody.* San Jose, CA. 1976. Pg. 2.

2. *Webster's New World Dictionary.* College Ed. World Pub. Co. N.Y. 1960. Pg. 289.

CHAPTER FIVE

1. Rodegast, Pat & Stanton, Judith. *Emmanuel's Book.* Bantam Books. 1987. Pg. 57.

2. Salzberg, Sharon. **Lovingkindness,** *The Revolutionary Art of Happiness.* Shambala. Boston. 1995. Pg. 18.

3. Ibid. Salzberg.

4. Gaskell, G.A. *Dictionary of All Scriptures and Myths.* Julian Press. N.Y. 1969. Pg. 283.

5. Ibid. Webster.

6. O'Keefe, Georgia. *Georgia O'Keefe.* Viking Press. 1978. Pg. 24.

CHAPTER SIX

1. Ausubel, Kenny. *Seeds of Change.* The Living Treasure. Harper. San Francisco. 1994. Pg. 1.

2. Hahn, Thich Nhat. *Peace Is Every Step.* Bantam. N.Y. 1992. Pgs. 73-75.

3. Ibid. Salzberg. Pg. 39.

4. Piburn, Sidney, ed. *The Dalai Lama, A Policy of Kindness.* Snow Lion Pub. N.Y. 1993. Pg. 79.

CHAPTER SEVEN

1. Kryon. *Alchemy of the Human Spirit.* Kryon Writings. Del Mar, CA. 1996. Pgs. 133-135.

2. Chopra, Depak. *The Way of the Wizard.* Harmony Books. N.Y. 1995. Pgs. 150-151.

3. Ibid. Kryon. Pg. 137.

4. Ibid. Kryon. Pg. 135.

CHAPTER EIGHT

1. Fincher, Susanne F. *Creating Mandalas.* Shambala. Boston. 1991. Pg. 134.

2. Ibid. Jung. Pg. 335.

3. Woodman, Marion. *Addition to Perfection.* Inner City Books. Toronto. 1982. Pg. 196.

4. Bly, Robert. *A Little Book on the Human Shadow.* Harper. San Francisco. 1988. Pg. 2.

5. Ibid. Pg. 17-20.

6. Ibid.

7. Ibid. Pg. 43.

8. Cameron, Julia. *The Artist's Way.* Tarcher/Perigee Books. N.Y. 1992. Pg. 27.

9. Gold, Peter. *Navajo and Tibetan Sacred Wisdom: The Circle of the Spirit.* Inner Traditions Int'l. Vermont. 1994. Pg. 1.

10. Ibid. Pg. 2.

11. Ibid. Pg. 298.

12. Khanna, Madhu. Yantra. *The Tantric Symbol of Cosmic Unity.* Thames & Hudson. London. 1997. Pg. 9.

13. Barendsen, Kristin. "Why People Don't Heal." *Yoga Journal.* Sept-Oct. 1996. Issue #130. Pg. 71.

14. Ibid. Cameron. Pg. 134.

CHAPTER NINE

1. Ibid. Jung. Pg. 196-199.

2. Brennan, Barbara Ann. *Hands of Light.* Bantam Books. N.Y. 1988. Pg. 269-70.

3. Ibid. Pg. 263.

CONCLUSION

1. Ibid. Jung. Pg. 342.

2. Eliot, T.S. *The Complete Poems and Plays 1901-1950.* Harcourt Brace & Co. N.Y. "Four Quartets; Little Gidding," Part V. Pg. 145.

3. Neihardt, John G. *Black Elk Speaks.* Washington Square Press. N.Y. 1972. Pg. 164.

I may not have written this book had it not been for the vision of Maggie Cheney. I thank her for encouraging me all the way. During Maggie's vision I was miles away chanting at a retreat and came away *knowing* I would be successful. Thank you Gurumayi. Thank you to John McCaffrey for the support in all the classes, including knowing that we should chant.

Thank you to all my students who trusted in me and the mandala process and suggested I put the process down on paper. I wish I could have included all your magnificent work. A very big thank you to all those who allowed me to use their artwork, the book could not have been done without it. Thank you to Don and Kim for crafting this book so beautifully.

Thank you to Maureen Forrester whose first mandalas inspired my first mandalas. Thank you to Gäel Roziére in whose bodywork sessions my mandala work began. Thank you to Donna Ostlund who helped me start acknowledging the darkness, to Joanne Young who helped me through it, and Lori Vainer who walked with me and taught me what it was to be a friend. Thank you to Noelle Takahashi who taught me about the energy in mandalas.

To my husband, Don Faia, I will be eternally grateful. He believed in me from the beginning and never wavered in his support and conviction that I was truly an artist—it took me a long time to believe him. Thank you to my mother-in-law Alice who so vehemently proclaimed my artistic ability while hiding her own. Thank you to my father for teaching me about growing things, and to my mother for her love of flowers which she passed on to me. Thank you to my eighth grade art teacher Don Maxwell who ignited my love of watercolor and acknowledged me as an artist.

And, finally, thank you to my dear friend Lane Cara Shaw, who loved mandala work, teaching it and teaching others how to teach it. She believed in me, encouraged the writing of this book and helped me in so many ways, and continues to do so. She passed away at 92 before she was able to see the book published. Her *Vision of the Future* below shows her belief that mandala work would be taught around the world. I am very grateful, in fact, to all my unseen teachers who have undoubtedly worked overtime assisting me! One was my grandmother who stood by me as I painted the cover mandala and said, "You can do it."

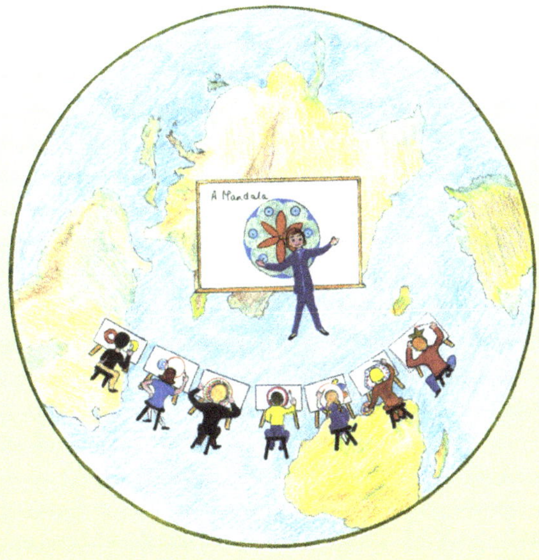

Lane Cara Shaw, *A Vision Of The Future*, watercolor, colored pencil

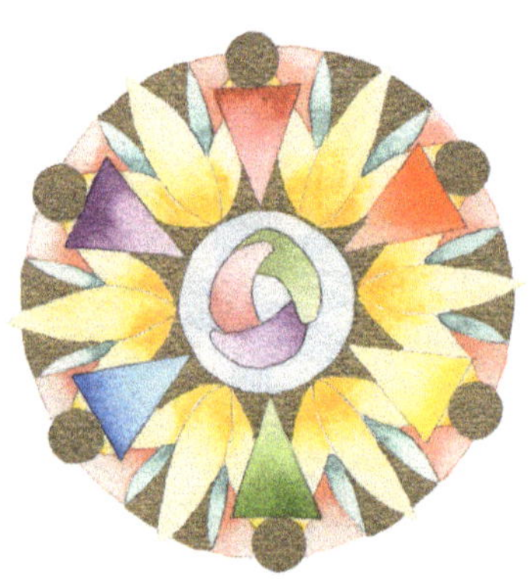

art as a path to the heart

MICHELE FAIA
classes and workshops
watercolor paintings

www.michelefaia.com